W9-AAH-014

SELLING

SELLING

BY LLOYD ALLARD
KING OF SALESMEN

PELICAN PUBLISHING COMPANY

Gretna 1991

Library of Congress Cataloging-in-Publication Data

Allard, Lloyd
    Selling/by Lloyd Allard.
      p. cm.
    ISBN 0-88289-849-3
    1. Selling. I. Title.
    HF5438.25.A438 1991
    658.8'5—dc20   91-12319
                       CIP

Published by Pelican Publishing Company, Inc.
1101 Monroe Street, Gretna, Louisiana 70053
Printed in Canada

Machiko*

A vision came from the Orient,
Mysterious and beautiful

She came in troubled times
Chaos reigned

Her smile lighted the recesses
Of my mind

Her healing hands soothed
My troubled brow

Her industry brought order
To the chaos of my home

Her kind, gentle disposition
Gave me peace

Her passion rekindled
My desire

Her love brought happiness
To my life

WELCOME DAUGHTER OF JAPAN.
LIVE WITH ME FOREVER.

(*Machiko is Japanese for "Welcome Daughter")

I would like to dedicate this book
to my lovely wife, Machiko,
and my good dog, Rex.

Contents

Foreword

I'm the guy that gave "The King" his crown. He'd earned it, he deserved it, and everything that I've seen before and since that "crowning" years ago has reaffirmed my opinion that Lloyd Allard is the world's greatest salesman.

Let's pause for a moment to permit me to present my credentials so that my introduction of "The King" and his book will have some credibility for those of you who do not know me. I joined Gulf Development, Inc. in August of 1965 at the age of twenty-five. We had about seven salespeople and we sold plastic outdoor signs to retail businesses. We grew and grew and kept on growing. We were fortunate to have a terrific owner-president, Kozell Boren, who put together a great staff, the best manufacturing facilities in the sign business, and a fantastic marketing system which sells our products through independent dealers who sell on a direct, one-call basis. We pride ourselves on having excellent products, standing behind them after the sale, and in having a well-trained, highly motivated sales force.

I have worn many hats through the years: manager of customer service, director of transportation, training director, vice president of sales, and, for the last five years, president. I retired at the age of fifty and bought a small ranch in the Texas Hill Country near Fredericksburg. Most of my years were spent recruiting, teaching, and managing salespeople. I've opened offices, recruited, and trained salespeople in every major city in the United States over the last twenty-five years. I know and love the Great American Salesmen, and Lloyd Allard is the best...period.

Now, back to the introduction of The King and his book. Actually, he should have two crowns. Lloyd holds most of the personal sales records at Gulf Development, Inc. He has the record for the highest dollar volume in a month, most personal contracts written, highest percentage of delivered business (100 percent), etc., etc. However, Lloyd is also the best sales manager I've ever met. He's a teacher who truly loves to share his talents with his salespeople.

We had a standing joke at our headquarters in Torrance, California that Lloyd's successes in sales and sales management could be explained by the simple fact that he was just "lucky." "Everywhere Lloyd goes," we would say, "people just happen to want to buy that day...or everywhere Lloyd goes people just happen to need a job that day and so they go to work with him." Lloyd's proudest accomplishment in personal sales is not the sales record he set that still stands 7 years later but the fact that 100 percent of his customers love him. His proudest accomplishment in sales management is not the regional sales records that he's set and still holds...but the fact that he's promoted more sales managers than any person in the history of our company.

The people in our world can be categorized into two camps. There are takers and there are givers. I call takers Quarter horses because they sometimes can do well in the short run on a fast track. Givers, on the other hand, are the real Thoroughbreds who have the endurance and stamina for the long run under any conditions.

Takers are small-minded, self-centered people who think mostly of themselves first in any given situation. Salespeople won't work for a taker very well or for very long. It doesn't take long for a salesperson to realize who and what a taker is really interested in. On the other hand, salespeople will go that extra mile, stay motivated, and work forever for a giver.

You see, a giver not only gives of his or her talents and time; he or she cares, and salespeople quickly see that. Think about it. Don't all the successful people you know fall into the "givers" category?

Lloyd is a giver. If he has a fault, it's being a soft touch for a down-and-out salesperson. In Lloyd's early days as a sales manager I had to caution him on several occasions about overextending himself for his people. He worked 7 days a week, loaned money, paid motel bills for his people, and so on to a point that I became concerned for his personal financial well-being. I was happy to hear that he had cut down on loans to his salespeople until I found out that he had stopped loaning money and was giving it away.

Don't get me wrong. The formula for successful sales management is not loaning or giving money to your people. It's the hundreds of other things that Lloyd does so well, including a deep concern for the mental, physical, and financial health of the people who choose to work for and with him. A true champion in sales and life who is worthy of "wearing the crown" and earning the title of "The King of Salesmen" has to have a lot of adjectives describing him. Only a few of them are: intelligent, motivated, loyal, caring, industrious, skillful, positive, tolerant...oh, yes...and lucky.

This talented professional teacher, speaker, sales manager, and salesman whom I call friend has all of these attributes and more. I recommend that you read and re-read his book...you'll be glad you did!

SAM GOLDEN

Preface

Selling is an ancient and honorable profession. Today, as throughout history, millions of people make their living by selling goods or services to others. When I was a poor boy working on a farm in the South, I had a dream that's shared by many people.... I dreamed of someday being successful. I wanted to travel, see the world, and make a lot of money. I thought I could do these things by being a salesman.

Later, when my life seemed to be crumbling to dust all around me, I decided it was time to put my dreams into action. I became a direct salesman. I've never regretted that decision.

I hope you enjoy reading my story. I also hope you'll learn something from it. Selling has given me much in recent years. It's my sincere desire to give something back to this profession that's done so much for me. I hope that this book can, in some small way, help serve that purpose.

Acknowledgments

I would especially like to thank Kozell Boren, whose genius and generosity made this book and my career in sales possible. As founder and president of Gulf Development, Kozy has made it possible for thousands of independent businesspeople and salespeople to live a richer life. Kozy is a genius whose ideas and inventions are always copied but never equaled, and he is one of those rare individuals who does everything well. Inventor, sportsman, world traveler, yachtsman, scuba diver, pilot, manufacturer, motivator, oilman, world-class skeet shooter, gourmet cook, salesman, and financial genius, Kozy excels in it all. It is a great honor for me to work with such an original thinker. It is a great honor and privilege to call Kozy Boren my friend. Also, I would like to say thank you to Joe Page, who graciously and skillfully lent his editorial expertise to this project.

Introduction

After much disappointment and failure in my life, I decided to become a direct salesman. This decision changed my life dramatically for the better. I would like to share with you that adventure and some of the things I have learned.

I made a commitment to study, work, and practice my trade until I was not only rich, but also recognized as the best direct salesman in America. Since that day in 1978, I've diligently read everything I could find about salesmanship. I've analyzed different ideas about selling, and practiced every sales technique that I thought might work. This commitment to the art of salesmanship has paid off. I've discovered many basic principles that are at the heart of the selling process. Those principles have changed my life. They might change yours, as well. I've also discovered that many popular ideas about selling are absolutely incorrect and even dangerous. I hope to set the record straight once and for all on many of those ideas.

Four key points can summarize my perspective on selling, and illustrate why I decided to write this book.

First, the principles of selling that I've learned over the years *really work.* A description of these principles, and "real life" stories that illustrate these principles in action, make up the core of this text. All of these principles are rock solid, and have been proven in the field. Any salesperson who learns these principles and works hard to apply them will succeed.

Second, most of the sales techniques and principles being taught today are nothing but junk. Frequently their primary objective is not to help you sell better, but to sell *you* the books, audiocassettes, or seminars that present the techniques.

Third, because of the many opportunities offered by this profession, it attracts certain people who want to take advantage of those opportunities and the people who pursue those opportunities. There are parasites and con men who make their livings trying to exploit salespeople. Many "sales opportunities" advertised today are, in fact, thinly disguised pyramid schemes in which the salesperson must buy a product before he or she can sell it. Many of the people in charge of such a scheme suck the juice out of thousands of honest salespeople, who wind up with nothing. Armed with the knowledge contained in this book, you need never fall prey to these vultures.

Finally, I believe that being a salesman can be the most exciting and rewarding job on earth. By sharing my experiences and my ideas, I hope to share my enthusiasm about salesmanship and help others become successful sales professionals. I would like to draw attention to what I consider the world's greatest profession: selling.

SELLING

CHAPTER 1

My Story

It is easy for me to pinpoint the darkest, most awful time of my life. That time was July of 1978. I'd lost everything that had ever been important to me. All my life I'd been a hard worker and a good provider. I was a dedicated churchgoer who taught classes at Sunday school. I preached at the local Rescue Mission. I had a wife, children, and a big home with a swimming pool in the yard. I bought a new car almost every year. I took pride in the fact that I was never late paying a bill. My children went to a private school, and I had many good friends. From the outside my life seemed perfect. It looked as though I had it all.

Then everything started to unravel. As she had threatened to do for many years, my wife filed for a divorce. I'd always thought of divorce as something that only happened to losers. It *couldn't* happen to me! I fought vigorously to save the life I had. It seemed impossible to me that I'd no longer be able to raise my children the way I'd planned. Despite all my best efforts, I failed. After the divorce, I felt lost and confused. My faith in God, which had always been such an important force in my life, was slipping away. I felt like a ship that had lost its rudder.

I decided to fight my way back by marrying the first attractive woman I could find that was available. This, I thought, would show everyone that I wasn't a loser. I soon remarried. It ended abruptly after a disastrous five months. Not long after this second divorce, I lost my job and quickly fell into debt. My car was repossessed. I was forced to move into a squalid basement apartment in an abandoned house. My sister died suddenly, and I was so broke that I couldn't afford the travel costs to attend her funeral.

One by one, my friends abandoned me. None of the many people I'd helped over the years offered assistance, or even a kind word. I soon became very bitter and angry. I believed that I'd done my best to be a good husband, father, and member of the community. Now I felt as though I was being rejected by everyone—by my family, friends, and worst of all by God. In bitterness, I cursed God. I remember walking for hours through cold rain, mocking God and asking Him to give me pneumonia and put an end to my misery by letting me die.

My apartment was a dark and miserable place. Cobwebs hung down from overhead pipes, and mildew clung to the walls. The dim lights cast a ghostly glow across the cold, concrete floor. I was now driving an old, orange pickup truck with over a hundred thousand miles on the odometer. It seemed to stop running every time I'd hit a bump in the road. The starter burned out regularly and I was too broke to have it repaired.

My situation was maddening. Everything was wrong. It seemed as though everyone wanted money from me—money I didn't have to give. I heard plenty of criticism from people I'd thought were my friends. Everyone who knew me seemed to think that I was down for the count.

Sometimes, even during this terrible time, I'd bitterly smile to myself, thinking that I'd surely be back on top some day. But when? And how? There seemed to be no way out. Soon I was down to one last possession of any real value. One night, I put my Smith and Wesson revolver under my jacket and walked into town. I knew that this gun was worth several hundred dollars. I sold it for fifty. As I pocketed that money, I realized that when it was gone, I'd have nothing. I was, indeed, in a pit—a deep, desolate pit that I'd dug for myself.

ENLIGHTENMENT

I shall never forget the morning of my enlightenment, either. As I lay in my untidy bed one morning, I stared blankly up at my dirty basement window. Unsettled thoughts drifted in and out of my mind. Suddenly, I was gripped by a simple but compelling question. Is this how I'll have to spend the rest of my life? The thought stunned me like a hard punch to the stomach. It was like an electric shock.

First fear and then anger welled up inside me. I sat bolt upright in the bed and shouted, "No, this is the end of my *old* life! It's the beginning of my *new* life!" Suddenly a new excitement and warmth flowed through me. I felt reborn...everything seemed possible. As I sat there in the bed, I daydreamed about all the things I'd do, and I made some important decisions.

First and foremost, I decided to do exactly what I wanted to do, regardless of anyone else's opinions. For the first time in my life I felt free of the shackles of the necessity of pleasing others. I didn't give a damn what anyone thought or said about me. This time, I'd do things *my* way. I then promised myself to become a master of whatever I decided to do. I was determined to find out just how good I could be at something. I decided to show the world that Lloyd Allard really *was* a winner.

The change was not as important as the conversion of Paul, but it was certainly as unexpected. I felt like Alice in Wonderland. Through my mind's eye I had entered into a new land where anything was possible.

It's amazing what a simple change in perspective can do for a person. I immediately started thinking about what I wanted to do for the rest of my life. I began planning for my future. One thought soon pushed itself to the front of my mind. Many years earlier, I'd read a book about a fellow named Bettinger who'd made a lot of money as a direct salesman. I had always been fascinated by the lifestyle, the freedom, and the profit potential available to travelling salesmen. The more I thought about this possibility, the more excited I became. Why not? Why not become a salesman? In fact, why not become the world's *best* salesman?

THE JOB

I knew enough about myself to know that having truly set out on a course, I would not stop until I reached my goals. It was time to act. I picked up a newspaper and turned eagerly to the want ads. Fate must have guided my eyes to the right spot on the page that day. The first ad I read promised from six hundred to a thousand dollars a week for successful direct salespeople. That seemed like a great place to start. I quickly dressed and went to see the man who'd placed the advertisement.

I arrived at the motel where the interviews were being conducted. I introduced myself to the interviewer, a big, well-dressed Southern gentleman named Art Murphy. As we started conversing, his tone and attitude soon told me that I wasn't making a very good first impression. Today, I remember every detail of that interview. My most vivid memory is of the steaming coffee he poured from a thermos into his ceramic cup. I sure could have used a cup of coffee just then. He didn't offer any.

Our discussion took a more promising turn when the man showed me the product his company sold. His firm, Gulf Sign Company, manufactured lighted signs for independent businesses. The owners of the company had invented a unique process for manufacturing and mass producing custom signs. The Gulf process made it possible for small, independent businesses to have high-quality exterior signs that rivalled the quality and eye appeal of large chain stores or franchises...at a *very* affordable price.

As he went on, I realized that this company's owner was a manufacturing and marketing genius. Not only had he developed a unique product that met a specific need in the marketplace, but he'd also devised a marketing technique that enabled salespeople to sell his signs on a one-call basis.

I became very excited. I loved the product, the process, and the sales approach. I was electrified by the whole program. "I can sell that!" I said. "That's it. That's what I want to do for the rest of my life. I'll get rich selling those signs!" My interviewer shook his head and smiled weakly as we shook hands and agreed to meet again the next day. I thought to myself, He doesn't seem to have been impressed with what he's seen.

That impression must have been reinforced the next morning when I pulled up in front of his house in my dilapidated orange truck. Later, as he handed me the sample sign and order forms, he made a passing comment that I'll always remember. "You know," he said, "you've got two chances to succeed—slim and none. And I think slim just left." I loved it. It stimulated my reawakening competitive spirit. I just smiled and thanked him for his "encouragement." I told him that all I needed at this point was the sample, the order pads, and a chance.

I hopped into the cab of my truck and leaned out the window to say good-bye. As I started the engine, I shouted one last comment to my new employer. "You know, Boss, you're going to be working for me some day!" He laughed loudly as I pulled away from his house.

PREPARING TO BE A SALESMAN

During the drive home, I thought about how I was going to sell this product. Where should I start? What should I do? The same doubts, fears, and hopes that are shared by most prospective salesmen were rushing through my mind.

I found myself hurriedly scribbling ideas for my presentation on a scrap of paper. When I got back to my apartment, I organized my thoughts and wrote out my sales presentation. I was too excited to eat or even sleep. I studied and rehearsed my presentation *all* night. This was the beginning of a self-made course of study and practice in direct sales that I've continued to this very day.

IN THE FIELD

I practiced my presentation and studied my product for three days. I hardly slept or ate. Finally, I was ready. I put on my last suit and went out looking for my first prospect. It didn't take long before I noticed a small, unimposing auto body shop located just four blocks from my apartment. The humble exterior of the shop cried out for a new sign. I walked in. I had the strange feeling that this call would represent the total of my new career in sales.

The owner, a husky fellow named Bob, was busily poring over a desk full of paperwork as I approached him. I got his attention and shook his hand vigorously. "Hi!" I said. "I'm Lloyd Allard, vice-president of Gulf Sign Company. I have a new product that will make you a lot of money. I would like to show it to you, okay?"

Bob leaned back in his chair. "No, don't bother." He pointed toward one corner of his shop. "I'm almost finished making my own sign, see? It's right over there." I caught sight of a young man in the corner carefully painting the border of a shiny new metal sign. It was almost finished. My heart sank, but I decided to press on. "Tell you what, Bob. Let me show you what you should have bought, O.K.?" Bob shrugged. "All right, if you want to," he said with a friendly smile. "I'm ready for a break from this paperwork, anyway."

I plugged in my sample sign. Magic happened. Suddenly, I had Bob dreaming about a large, lighted sign with his name on it. Others in the shop started noticing me, and came over to hear what I had to say. Soon they became active participants in my presentation. As they asked questions, they became more and more involved, and started to share Bob's excitement. I solicited their approval for my proposal. It soon became apparent that these onlookers were actually helping me make the sale!

Bob quickly forgot about his metal sign. When I asked for the order, he didn't hesitate for a moment. As I wrote the contract, Bob wrote me a check for four hundred dollars. I had done it!

Since this deposit was my commission for the sale, I'd just earned four hundred dollars in my first hour as a direct salesman!

I wanted to rush to the bank to cash my check, but Bob wanted to talk for a while longer about his new sign. After a short while, I said my good-byes and prepared to leave. Bob offered to carry my sample sign to my car. He still had more to tell me about his business, and more questions to ask me about that new sign.

As we walked up to my old, battered truck, Bob stopped in his tracks and stared. After a brief pause, he said, "Wait a minute. If you're the vice-president of the company, why are you driving around in this old thing?" I had to think fast. After all, the image I'd created—an image of success and competence—had been part of the reason for my success. This truck certainly did nothing to support that image.

"Yeah, isn't that something?" I said. "This is what the darn rental company stuck me with. I'm never going there again! Oh, by the way...how do I get to your bank?" After my new customer cheerfully gave me directions to his bank, I headed there and cashed the check. The next stops were a clothing store and a car rental agency. Two new suits and one shiny new rental car later, I looked like the successful salesman I was determined to become.

That night I went over everything I did to analyze why I was able to make the sale. The next day, I tried again in a different town. First I called on a car dealership. No sale. Next, a motorcycle shop. Five partners listened to my presentation and then debated among themselves before making their decision. Yes, they finally agreed, they'd take it! This second sale meant that I now had another four hundred dollars of commission in my pocket.

From my first day in the field, I practiced my presentation again and again until I could deliver it perfectly. I experimented with different sales approaches as I gained more experience. I tried out everything that seemed even the least bit reasonable. I decided I should test the limits of my credibility. I didn't care what the customer thought about me or said to me. This sometimes led to some flamboyant presentations, but I didn't let occasional outrageousness stand in my way. One of my mottos became "Don't worry…they won't hit an idiot!" Once I had freed myself from worry about what people would think of me, I was able to try anything. I made careful notes outlining the pros and cons of every technique I tried. I analyzed which were effective and which were not. Soon I had fine-tuned my sales presentation to the point where I could sell to almost anyone.

My basic approach focused attention on the *customers'* self-image. I *knew* that the product I was offering could help many businesses grow and prosper. I believed that when I failed to sell a customer, I'd failed to *help* him. Once I'd fixed that attitude in my mind, I was determined to sell to everyone.

My next customer had already been approached by one of the managers of our company, with no success. When I first spoke with him, he peppered me with a barrage of reasons why he didn't want to buy—reasons he'd thought up during the manager's earlier visit. I knew this wouldn't be an easy sale.

Regardless of this resistance, I believed firmly that this customer *deserved* the benefits our sign could offer. To help him understand that, I had to build value for the customer. He had to understand what the sign would do for him, and how it would improve his business. At the same time, I tried to rekindle his dream. This simply means that I helped the customer rediscover the feelings, the excitement, and the hope he had when he first went into business. All too often, the struggles of day-to-day living can smother those feelings. I knew all about that, and my job, as I saw it and see it, was to uncover them and let them burn brightly once again.

I helped my customer visualize the lighted sign with his name prominently displayed as it glowed brightly above his shop on Calumet Avenue. I let him visualize his friends looking at the sign…new customers being attracted by the sign, then coming into his shop and spending their money. Suddenly, the magic happened once again. His objections dissolved. The money was available for the purchase. In fact, he said, he'd been planning to buy a sign all along! He patted me on the back and told me how lucky I was to walk into his shop at just the right moment to make the sale!

You know, it's strange how lucky I've been all these years. I seem to have an amazing knack for walking into a business at the exact moment the owner of that business is ready to make the decision to buy an exterior sign!

ON THE ROAD

After one month of successful selling, I was ready for my first real adventure…and for earning some serious money. At the end of my first month I sold a sign to a car dealership. I gave him a fantastic deal on a sign, and he gave me a fantastic deal on a car. I had a dream. That dream had been to travel, sell, see the world, and make unlimited amounts of money. I packed my suitcase, tossed it into my new car, and headed south from Hammond, Indiana. I carried just one five-dollar bill in my pocket.

I began selling signs throughout Indiana, Ohio, Kentucky, West Virginia, and Tennessee. During the early part of this trip, I discovered another interesting fact about sales. The idea is simple: if customers see *you* with a lot of money, *they* tend to feel more prosperous, and are more likely to buy. Also, when your customers see that you have a lot of money, they're reassured that you're not after theirs.

That first trip was a spectacular success. When I returned home, I counted the cash I'd collected. I had over ten thousand dollars in hundred-dollar bills. As I stared at the money, I realized that now, for the first time in my life, I was totally free.

LEARNING TO SELL

As I travelled, I mentally reviewed every successful sales call I made. I analyzed my presentation, examining what had worked and what hadn't. The old cliché says that you learn from your mistakes. Actually you don't. You learn by doing things *right,* and then doing them again and again, improving on your successes as you go.

As I travelled throughout the country, I soon learned another simple truth—namely, that people are essentially very much alike, regardless of where they live or what they do. No matter what their social position, education, or financial status, people everywhere respond either positively or negatively to the same things in the same ways.

I've sold from Nome, Alaska to Columbus, Georgia, from San Francisco and Los Angeles to Boston and New York City. I've never found a dime's worth of difference in people. When correct sales principles are applied correctly, they work—everywhere, and with everyone.

Other basic truths became clear to me right away. First, everybody wants to do business with a true professional. If you look extremely successful, people pay more attention to you and treat you with more respect. Soon I was wearing expensive clothing and driving a new Lincoln Continental. I created an image of wealth and success that made selling easier for me.

Second, people feel more at ease when they know they're doing business with someone who knows what he's doing. One of the best qualifications for a salesperson is not a glib tongue, but self-confidence. If you have confidence in yourself, your customers will find it easy to have confidence in you.

Still another important lesson that has made me hundreds of thousands of dollars is a simple but profound one. Millions of people out there desperately need to have someone rekindle their dreams. These people have been beaten and broken by the "real world." They've been forced to compromise their dreams by the day-to-day necessities of earning a living. If you can cause these people to see that dream once again, and then incorporate your product into those rekindled dreams, you can sell anything.

AN ADVENTURE

I spent my first winter as a salesman in Atlanta, Georgia. I enjoy being around Southerners, and I sure wanted to get away from the cold northern winter. During this winter, I had more fun and earned more money than I ever had before. A typical sale went something like this:

I'd pull the long nose of my Lincoln up to the door of a redneck bar and walk in slowly, wearing a thousand-dollar suit and several thousands worth of jewelry. I'd walk slowly to the center of the room and raise my hand, on which gleamed an expensive ring. I would stand there, hand raised, until every head in the room was turned in my direction. A hushed silence would fall over the room. "Who's the owner of this bar?" I'd ask. When the owner identified himself, I would say, "I have something that'll make you rich! I'd like to show it to you, O.K.?"

I'd often include all the patrons in on the selling process. I'd soon have them all agreeing that the owner really needed a new sign. It was easy for all the customers to buy into my proposal. They could afford to be "big spenders"—after all, this sale wasn't going to cost *them* a dime! I'd often have the customers vote on my offer. Should he or shouldn't the owner buy? It'd be hard for the owner to say no when all the customers and employees in the place were encouraging him to go ahead and buy. At the same time, it would be easy for him to justify the purchase when all his friends were telling him that buying a new sign was the logical thing to do. As I perfected my technique, selling became easy, and the money came rolling in.

THE PROMOTION

In the spring, my employer contacted me and praised me on my progress. He then asked if I'd be interested in a new challenge—a promotion to the position of District Manager. I wasn't thrilled with the prospect at first. "No," I said, "I'm having too much fun selling!" Then he dangled the carrot. "You know, you can make a 6 percent commission on the sales volume of everyone you hire." I smiled and said, "Well, in that case…" Later, however, I began to wonder if I'd be able to teach other salespeople the sales techniques that I'd been developing.

That evening, I met a man named Clyde at the supermarket. Clyde was a farmer from Kentucky who'd recently been making his living hanging drywall. I asked him if he'd be interested in becoming a salesman. He shook his head and said, "Hell, I couldn't sell anything." I was eager to get started in my new role, so I coaxed him into coming with me and watching me make a sale the next day. He shrugged and decided to head out with me. He figured he had nothing to lose.

One sale later, Clyde was hooked. I had made it look so easy that he figured anyone could do it. First I taught him the presentation and then I dressed him up like a professional salesman. His first sale was unforgettable. After his call, he swaggered into the restaurant where we were to meet, threw down the money and the completed order form onto the table, and let out a loud war whoop. "So, how'd it go, Clyde?" I asked. "Did you have any problems?" "Just one," he said. "You know that part where you ask for the order? Well, I forgot what I was supposed to say." "So what did you do?" I asked. "Well, that fellow finally asked me how he could get one of those signs, and I said, 'Mister, money talks, and you ain't said jack!'"

Clyde became the second highest volume salesman in our company. His story is just one of the exciting and rewarding experiences I've had hiring and training people. Many of these are people who would never have succeeded if they hadn't decided to enter the world's most exciting profession—sales.

I've hired taxi drivers, dish washers, schoolteachers, and farmers. I've hired people with little or no education, and people with doctoral degrees. Some of those people are now earning between twenty and thirty thousand dollars…a *month!* Any person who makes a commitment to work hard and to learn the principles of selling outlined in this book *will* succeed in sales, regardless of their background or education.

BIG MACK

Many of the prospective salespeople I've hired and trained over the years have seemed like unlikely candidates for success. Perhaps the most unlikely of them all was a burly fellow called Big Mack. Mack measured six feet, six inches tall and weighed in at three hundred pounds. He was a raw, gruff redneck from Arkansas who chewed tobacco and wore old Levis and a dirty t-shirt every day of his life.

I began Mack's field training in the company of another experienced salesman. After he watched me make my first sale, I suggested that Mack and the other salesman flip to see which of them would get credit for the order. As I turned to speak with the customer, I heard the other salesman yelling at the top of his lungs. I looked around and my jaw dropped. There was Mack, holding his well-dressed companion high over his head. He smiled and said, "So, how far do you want me to flip him, boss?"

Mack, along with several other new salespeople, quickly learned the ins and outs of selling, and soon my little district was outselling big regions with four or five separate districts. A few months later, I was asked by my boss to move to our main office in California to teach my techniques to other salespeople. Once again, I didn't want to give up the job I was enjoying so much. Once again, the company found a way to sweeten the pot. My boss said, "You know, if you take this position, you could make fifteen percent commission on every sale in the region!" I didn't need to understand higher math to know what kind of profit potential that would mean. I said, "O.K., sure...I'll do it!"

IN LOS ANGELES — JIMMY THUMPER

I went to Los Angeles burning up to find out if I could make it in a big city. At first, I didn't know if I'd have a chance to find out. The manager wanted me to be properly "indoctrinated" into the L.A. way of doing things. He wanted me to spend two weeks in the office. Well, I've never had much use for offices...I like to sell. There was just one thing for me to do.

During my lunch break on that first day in the office, I slipped out to make a call. By two o'clock, I was cashing an eight hundred-dollar commission check. That ended my management training.

But managing involved more than selling, and I needed to get my staff lined up. I hired some local salespeople, and things started off fairly well. Still, I sensed that something was missing. I was selling well myself, but no matter how much money I made, my sales people weren't impressed. My success wasn't enough to motivate them. By this time, they simply *expected* me to sell well. They wanted to see one of *them* tearing up the territory and making a lot of money. I needed someone who could build excitement in my sales force by demonstrating the potential offered by the job. I needed someone who could make successful selling look easy. I needed what we call a "spiz man."

One bright California morning, as we sat drinking coffee in the Los Angeles airport Holiday Inn, my "spiz man" walked into my life. I knew he was the man I was looking for immediately. He was self-confident, quick, clever, crafty, and street wise. Later I learned that one of my salespeople had tried to sell him a sign for his used car lot. He was apparently more intrigued by the salesman's presentation than the product he was offering, and told the salesman that he wanted to see the man who'd hired him. And now, here he was.

He walked up to my table. "You Allard?" he asked. I looked him in the eye and smiled. "Yes...and you're my new 'spiz man.' I'm going to dress you up like Diamond Jim Brady and teach you how to sell signs. I'm going to make you rich, and you're going to make me famous. Now, sit down and have some breakfast." Without another word he joined my team.

His name was Jim. We called him "Jimmy Thumper" because of his tendency to...well, to thump people! Jimmy had a temper that he sometimes just couldn't control. He broke another salesman's nose once...in the middle of a sales meeting! But Big Jim turned out to be one of the best direct salesmen I've ever met. We travelled together all over the United States selling signs with spectacular success.

Even we were impressed with how well we did turning what appeared to be impossible situations into sales. Once, we decided to try our hand in a bar and restaurant that had a large FOR SALE sign mounted in the front window. The owner turned out to be a tough, older woman who wasn't in a very good mood. After we introduced ourselves and I started my pitch, she said, "You boys are sure some kind of fools trying to sell me a sign. Can't you read that sign? I'm gonna sell this place and retire." She pointed to the FOR SALE sign.

Well, we sold her a sign. Not only did we make the sale, but we also talked her into taking her business off the market, remodeling the lounge, and making another go of it. As her dreams came back to life, she became excited about all of her new possibilities—possibilities that she simply hadn't been able to visualize for herself. Later she got on the phone and raised Cain with the real estate representative who'd first suggested she sell her business.

I loved my salespeople. I still do. They are my heroes. Salespeople are the most interesting, generous, and creative people on earth. I had an ironclad agreement with all of the salespeople who worked for me. I pledged to them that if they ever needed help, I'd go out with them, day or night, and help them sell and make money. I've sold signs at two or three o'clock in the morning. I've sold on every holiday of the year. I even went out on Christmas Day and made a thousand dollars just to prove that I could do it.

I managed the region in Los Angeles for two and a half years. During that time, my region was the number one sales performer for every month I was there. Then I grew restless again and was ready for a new adventure. I decided to take on the challenge of opening a new region in a tough market—New York City. No one from our company had ever done well in New York. This would be a great place to test and prove my sales techniques.

BREAKING RECORDS

Before I left for New York, I wanted to find out just how much my skill as a salesman had improved during my stint in L.A. I had an itch to get out there and sell again on my own. I took a month off from my job as a manager to really test the limits. I wanted to find out just how much money I could make as a salesman in one month.

When I first started with the company, our most successful salesman in the nation had achieved a total sales volume of thirty-nine thousand dollars for a month. After one month of hard-driving salesmanship using the principles I'd discovered, I sold one hundred and eleven thousand dollars in volume, and earned forty-two thousand dollars in commission in one calendar month on my own personal sales. I was definitely improving my skills as a salesman.

IN NEW YORK

I knew right from the start that New York City would be a challenge. To take on this challenge, I'd have to give up my successful region in Los Angeles which was now paying me about twenty thousand dollars a month. My prospects for success weren't very good. Three other managers had tried and failed to build a region there. Two of them flew out to Los Angeles to warn me against the move. I wanted to go to New York for one reason. I believed sound selling principles would work anywhere under any conditions. I wanted to test and prove my selling principles.

My friends tried everything to keep me from making this mistake. "Those New York hustlers will eat you alive," they told me. "You talk too slowly. They won't listen to your b.s. in New York." I smiled and nodded at them...but I knew what I wanted to do.

Shortly after flying into Kennedy Airport I ran an ad in the *New York Times*. I interviewed my first few salesmen at the airport's International Hotel. As soon as I felt we were ready, I took two of them up to 135th Street to begin my New York adventure. Despite all the warnings, the signs sold—and sold well! Soon I'd done something that had never been done before in our company. Starting from zero with no base and no staff in a new and hostile territory, I developed New York City into the number one sales region during the *first* month. And that was just the beginning. During the next three years, we broke almost every record the company had!

The lifestyle and culture of New York City were quite an experience for a small-town boy like me. I overdid everything, and I loved every minute of it. The salesmen in New York were something else, too. They all dressed like millionaires...and they tried hard to act the part!

Every morning, I bought breakfast for my salesmen and had a brief sales meeting with them. At first, before those people got to know me, those meetings weren't always easy to manage. I remember one morning in particular when I walked into our regular breakfast spot after a hard night of...well, let's just call it "New York culture." All I wanted was a strong cup of coffee and a good leaving alone. I saw the waitress talking to one of my managers. I waited about half a minute, but quickly grew impatient. I wanted my coffee.

The other salesmen were all shooting the bull. They looked as though they were ready to take on the world in their thousand-dollar suits and Gucci shoes. They hadn't even noticed that I'd come in. I decided to do something dramatic to get their attention...and to make a point. Any sales manager in charge of a group of direct salespeople never has much time to make an impression, and I was in a hurry. I believed that their success in the field depended on them hearing what I had to say. Besides, I wanted my coffee. I waited for about thirty more seconds. Finally, in a loud, harsh voice, I shouted, "Hey, get over here!" to the waitress.

The room fell completely silent. I looked around and saw that I had the undivided attention of thirty sharply dressed salesmen. Slowly and deliberately I stood up and said, "French toast, two eggs on top, and pour on a lot of syrup..." I paused and looked around the room, "...*for thirty people.*" Silence again. I looked from face to face. No one spoke. Everyone ate the breakfast I had ordered for them. A short while later, the district manager said to me, "Allard, I've heard some fantastic things about you, and now I believe them. That was the most astounding example of control I've ever seen. No one even complained about you ordering their breakfast."

Now, that might appear to be in bad taste, but if you never try something, how do you know if it will work? In selling, training, and teaching, the control of others is very important. You should master the control of others with your voice inflection, actions, and gestures. By the way, if you've never tried French toast with eggs and syrup, don't knock it. It's a Southern delicacy!

New York was a fantastic adventure from start to finish. Sometimes, just for fun, I'd go downtown and try out some new approaches. One of my favorites went something like this: I'd walk into a business and find the owner. In the slowest, thickest Southern drawl I could call up, I'd say something like, "Mister, will you please help me? They sent me up here from Kentucky to sell signs, but I must talk too slow, or something...no one'll listen to me. I got a heck of a deal for someone, but no one'll pay any attention to me. Would you please tell me what I'm doing wrong?" They'd sit me down, and after a short time, I'd sell a sign. Then they would tell me I'd better get tough or I wouldn't make it in New York.

All my friends told me that New York City would change me. I'd always answer by saying, "I came here to change New York...not to be changed by it!" Well, when New York and I parted company, neither of us had really changed that much. It was probably best for both of us that way.

CITY LIFE

One very important thing did change for me in New York, however. It all started when I tried to make a few creative adjustments to my domestic lifestyle. I had a large house with all the necessary appliances, but without all the necessary supplies. I've never been very good at domestic chores, and one day that fact caught up with me.

I had to do my laundry. I looked into every cabinet in the place, but couldn't find a trace of detergent anywhere. I did, however, find a can of Ajax cleanser. Well, soap is soap, I figured. I went ahead and did the wash, cleanser and all. You can probably imagine what happened next. A few days later I developed a most uncomfortable rash. I didn't put two and two together right away, so I imagined the worst.

I went to a doctor right away. He examined my rash, stood up, looked me in the eye, grinned, and said, "Just what the hell have you been washing your shorts in, my friend?" I said, "Doc, that is the nicest thing anyone ever said to me." I told him about the detergent and the mystery of the rash was solved.

The best part of this visit came a short while later when I met the doctor's charming Japanese nurse. We struck up a conversation, and the next thing I knew, I had a date! You must realize that this was no small accomplishment. After all, nurses have a reputation for being hard to impress. They've seen everything! Well, that visit to the doctor turned out to be a real stroke of fortune. That nurse is now my wife, Mrs. Machiko Allard, and this book is dedicated to her.

After I'd established the New York region and was sure that it was up and running, I moved on to Boston. There I hired a few salespeople, including a former teacher whom I taught to sell. That teacher is now my top manager in the nation. He's earning $25,000 a month—more than many teachers make in a year. I then went to a series of different cities to set up new regions. These included Columbus, Ohio; Indianapolis, Indiana; Memphis, Tennessee; Chicago, Illinois; and many others.

My pattern was the same. I'd place an ad in the local paper, then hire and train some salespeople. Later, I'd promote the top seller to the position of regional manager. Once I was satisfied that the region was operating effectively, I'd move on and set up a region somewhere else. In the last few years I have hired and trained hundreds of salespeople and managers. These people are living the American Dream of adventure and unlimited opportunity through direct sales. I have developed twenty-three regions in the northeast quarter of the United States. Recently I moved to New Orleans, Louisiana, where I intend to settle down and build regions throughout the South.

For me selling has always been magical. On 95th Street in Chicago or in the beautiful hills of Tennessee, in Los Angeles or New York, in Columbus, Georgia, or in Sitka, Alaska…you're always just one call away from adventure. Everyone I meet has a story to tell, and everyone has their own special plans and dreams.

I've never had what could be called a "bad day" in sales, and I've never met a customer I didn't like or didn't want to help. I've met very few people who didn't feel the same way about me. I've had more successes, made more money, seen more of the country, and helped more people in direct sales than I could have in any other profession.

MY CREDENTIALS

If someone writes a medical book, you would assume he or she has a background in medicine. If someone teaches law, you would think he or she probably has a legal background. However, there are hundreds of sales books, tapes, and seminars on the market that were written by people who are not salespeople. They do not understand salespeople or the selling process. Their theories sound good, so they write them down and teach or sell them. Salespeople read the books, listen to the tapes, and go to the seminars hoping to find something that will make them more effective at selling.

I have often heard people say, "If I get one good idea from this book, tape, or seminar, it will be worthwhile." Nothing could be farther from the truth.

I like Oreo cookies, but it would be unwise for me to jump into a sewer to get one. The bad stuff I would consume would do me more harm than the cookie would do me good. The bad ideas and misinformation you get by listening to someone who doesn't know their business is harmful also. If you are smart enough to always be able to tell the difference, you probably don't need the information. You already know it. The techniques I teach were learned in the field, and my credentials are that I made them work and taught them to others who make a lot of money using them.

When I started out in direct sales, the typical salesman in our business made one sale for every twenty calls he made. For every twenty calls I make, I make fourteen to sixteen sales. During my first year I made $105,000; my income went up to $220,000 the next year.

Ever since then, I've taken in from three hundred to four hundred thousand dollars every year. I've won trips to Las Vegas, Cancun, Hawaii, Jamaica, Alaska, and more. I've rafted on the white waters of the Snake River in Wyoming and sailed up the Mississippi on the *Mississippi Queen*. I've won every imaginable prize for sales performance, from gold coins, fur coats, and diamonds to plaques and trophies. Competing with hundreds of successful, competitive salesmen, I have set records in sales that have stood for years unchallenged.

I've learned that effective salespeople can live the good life if they're willing to work. I've marvelled at the freedom, the adventure, and the limitless opportunities that are available to direct salespeople. I've loved every minute I've spent in this business from the first faltering days when I needed a sale to pay for my motel room to the present day. I believe if any salesperson will combine the principles in this book with a lot of hard work, he or she will get rich.

CHAPTER 2

Exploring the Myths of Selling

Every year, salespeople spend millions of dollars on books, videotapes, and seminars that advocate unsound sales principles. Some of the ideas these programs present are merely silly. Others can be very harmful.

As salespeople, we have to be every bit as concerned about the teaching of unsound ideas about our profession as doctors and lawyers are about theirs. In this section, we will take a critical look at some of the more popular ideas being advanced today, and examine why they are incorrect and improper in the real-life world of selling. We will also examine the impact that these ideas can have on the success or failure of today's professional salespeople.

MYTH 1: "THE CUSTOMER IS ALWAYS RIGHT"

Probably the first idea most of us ever heard about selling was "the customer is always right." I remember hearing it as a young boy, and I'm certain I've run across it thousands of times since then. The theory behind this idea is simple: The salesperson should always agree with whatever the customer says or believes in order to make the sale.

When you examine this idea carefully, it is obviously illogical. In fact, it's so illogical that it's silly. Think, for example, how ridiculous this idea would sound if it were applied to any other profession. Consider the phrase "The patient is always right." You are sick and go to your doctor's office. You feel a little uneasy and uncertain, but you're sure the doctor will be able to help you. Instead, he looks you over, rubs his chin, and says, "Doggone, I don't know what the problem is. What do *you* think is wrong with you? What kind of medicine do *you* think I should prescribe?" Clearly, you would wonder about this doctor's qualifications…and you'd worry about what he might do to you! You'd much rather have a doctor who assures you that he knows what he is doing and knows what course of action to take.

How would you feel about an auto mechanic who said to you, "Say, I don't know what to do about your car…I've never heard a car sound like that! What do *you* think is wrong with it?"

You'd undoubtedly feel much more confident if he were to say, "If you want the car fixed right, I can fix it. If I can't do what needs to be done to fix a car correctly, I won't take the job."

Well, the same principle applies in selling. The truth is, customers are seldom right. In fact, they usually don't want or expect to be right. If they already knew all the answers they probably wouldn't want to spend their time talking with a salesperson in the first place!

When you speak with your customers, you share information about your area of expertise. You are a professional—someone who has something to share that will improve the customer's professional or personal life. If you let the customer know that *you* know what is best, and that you expect to do things the way they should be done, you have an excellent chance of making any sale.

Where's the harm, you may ask, in letting the customer think he's right? Why not just accommodate him, and do things his way? Well, the simple answer is that accommodating the customer is usually counterproductive. In our business, for example, we design the signs that our customers purchase. Quite often customers ask us to change a color, add words, or make other changes in the designs we propose. Many salespeople, anxious to make the sale, would jump at the chance to please the customer by making any changes, even needless or counterproductive ones, that were requested. The really good salesperson, however, will say, "No, this is how the sign should be designed. If I can't do it right, it won't help your business, and if it won't help your business, I don't want to do it. After all, my reputation is on the line here, too."

Salespeople who are too anxious to accommodate their customers usually accomplish only three things:

First, they let the customer see that they don't know what's best.

Second, they communicate the message that they don't really care what's best for the customer as long as they make the sale.

Third, the customer is left unsure of the wisdom of his or her purchase because he or she has to make some of the decisions. If the salesperson—the expert—isn't sure, how can the customer be sure?

The customer is seldom right, and the customer doesn't want to be right. The customer really wants to know only two things about a salesperson:

First, he or she wants to know that the salesperson knows what is best to help him or her meet a need.

Second, he or she wants to be sure that the salesperson has the integrity to do what is best. If you communicate those two facts about yourself to your customer, you can sell him or her almost anything.

SUMMARY: "THE CUSTOMER IS ALWAYS RIGHT"

The customer is not always right.
The customer does not want to be right.
The customer does not want the salesperson to try to make him think he is right.

The customer wants to do business with a salesperson who knows he or she is right.

The customer needs to know two things about the salesperson: that the salesperson knows what is right and that the salesperson has enough integrity to do what is right.

MYTH 2: "NEVER TELL THE CUSTOMER YOU'RE A SALESPERSON"

A while back, I attended a sales seminar in Los Angeles. It soon became obvious that the person leading the seminar had never sold much in his life…except sales seminars, I guess. If he had sold, he'd have understood just how far off the mark his ideas were. In fact, this seminar was so jam-packed with ridiculous notions that it inspired me to go ahead and write this book to set the record straight.

One of the principles proposed by the seminar leader went something like this: "Tell the customer you're a consultant, an adviser, or something else. Tell them you're doing a survey or conducting a poll. Tell them anything, but *never tell them you're a salesman!*"

As I glanced around the room, I saw the others attending this session nodding in agreement. I smiled to myself as I realized how much acceptance this absurd idea was getting. I turned to my good friend Sam Golden, who was attending the seminar with me. Sam had written the book *Selling As A Profession*, an excellent work that encourages salespeople to take pride in themselves and the work they do. I whispered to him, "Sam, this is pretty ridiculous, isn't it? I'm proud to be a salesman! I want everyone I meet to know I'm a salesman!"

The issue here is simple. Anyone who earns his or her income by selling products or services is a salesperson. If you ever tell a customer anything else, you're telling a lie. How can anyone expect salespeople to be honest with their employers and their customers if the first thing we teach them to do is tell their customers a lie?

How can a customer have confidence in anything a salesman says when it quickly becomes obvious that this person who claimed to be a consultant is, in fact, a salesman? Also, how can anyone be expected to develop pride in himself and his profession if he's taught to lie about it, as if it were something shameful and embarrassing?

A sale may be made *despite* the use of this tactic, but a sale will never be made *because* it's used. When you talk straight to your customers, treat them honestly, and take pride in what you do, you'll be much more successful than you'll ever be using deceitful strategies. You'll also have a longer career. Never deceive your customer and, more importantly, never deceive yourself.

When I was living in Yonkers, New York, I decided that I should buy another set of encyclopedias for myself. I never had an extensive formal education, so early in my life I developed the habit of looking things up whenever I needed information. One day an encyclopedia salesman appeared on my doorstep. He asked if he could show me his books. Well, this sure is a stroke of luck, I thought to myself. I want a set of encyclopedias, and here it is, walking through the door. I figured this young man was about to have one of his easiest sales ever. I invited him in.

Then he said it. "Now, before I start, I want to tell you that I'm not a salesman." I fumed. "Well, excuse me, but I want to buy a set of encyclopedias, so if you're not a salesman, you're wasting my time!"

He tried to recover his composure, and launched into his presentation. He was terrible. In fact, he did such a poor job that I finally stopped him in mid-sentence. I said, "O.K., you're right...I believe you. You are *not* a salesman! Go home and study your presentation until you are one, or send a real salesman over. I need some encyclopedias!" The poor kid sulked out the door, case in hand, and never returned. No one else ever showed up, either. Yes, yes, I know. I probably should have been more kind, but I'm just like everyone else. I don't like it when someone lies to me, and I dislike incompetency.

When that young man got back to his office without an order, he probably blamed his job, his territory, that S.O.B. who'd told him off, or maybe the selling profession in general. Everyone and everything else could be blamed. This viewpoint is one of the main reasons why some people become frustrated and move on to other careers. When you look closely at this frustration, it's plain to see that it has its roots in the perception that there is something wrong with being a salesman—that being a salesman is something to be hidden away from those to whom you want to sell.

Now, I can imagine an airplane pilot, a doctor, or a lawyer lying and telling folks they really are salesmen. But when I think about the opportunity, the adventure, and the money available in sales, I can't imagine any salesperson who'd want anyone to be in doubt about his or her profession. People always want to do business with real professionals, and that includes professional salespeople.

If you let your customers know from the start that you're a sales professional, the benefits can be enormous. An incident that occurred when I was based in Columbus, Ohio illustrates this clearly. One day, I was conversing with the owner of a boot store in his place of business. Bruce never hid the fact that he thought he was a very good salesman. His sales record backed up his opinion of himself.

Bruce was skeptical when I told him that I'd walk into businesses with no appointment, introduce myself, and sell a product for thousands of dollars within one hour. When I added that I'd collect a sizeable deposit which was my commission, have the customer make out the check in my name, and then direct me to his or her bank, Bruce simply didn't believe it. "No one's that good," he said. I asked Bruce if he would like to see me sell. Bruce shook his head, and then told me he'd have to see this for himself before he believed it. Bruce agreed to go watch me sell a sign.

We drove off in search of a customer. Soon we walked into a small auto repair garage and sought out the owner. George, the owner, was a friendly man, but he told us right off that we were too late to sell him a sign. He'd just bought one, he said. It was still packed in its crate in the storage room.

Bruce looked over at me with a slight grin. I thought quickly. "George, could I take a look at your new sign?" I asked. "Sure, no problem," he replied. He led the way as we walked off to the crammed storage room. As he pointed to the sign crate, I pulled a tape measure out of my pocket and started measuring the dimensions of the room.

George looked slightly worried. "What are you doing?" he asked. I answered, "Why, I'm measuring this room to see if you have room for another sign!" "But I don't want another sign," he stated flatly. "Yes, I know you don't," I responded. "But you see this fellow here? His name is Bruce. I told Bruce that I'm the best salesman in the world. I'm sorry, but I have to sell you a sign to prove to Bruce that I can sell to anybody. Now, I'll go and get my sample and try to sell to you. You do your best not to buy from me, o.k.?" George looked stunned. "Uhh...sure," was his only reply.

I had deliberately set up a nearly impossible situation...but I sold George a sign. I sold him the sign for two basic reasons. First, I really wanted to. Second, I'd studied and learned the principles that make selling easy. Bruce was so impressed with my performance that he sold his boot store and went to work for me.

If you earn a living in sales but aren't proud to call yourself a salesperson, you really should find another line of work. Both you and the sales profession will be happier in the long run with your decision.

SUMMARY: "NEVER TELL THE CUSTOMER YOU'RE A SALESPERSON"

Professional salespeople, like all other professionals, should take pride in their occupation.

Everyone wants to do business with a professional. Your customer wants to do business with a professional salesperson.

If you derive your income from the sale of a product or service, you are a salesperson, and to say otherwise is dishonest.

If you do not take pride in being a professional salesperson, you should find another occupation.

MYTH 3: "SUCCESS COMES FROM A POSITIVE MENTAL ATTITUDE"

In the past ten years, there have probably been more books written, more seminars given, and more tapes produced about this topic than any other. More wonderful benefits have been attributed to a positive mental attitude than to penicillin and *perestroika* combined. Today's salespeople are barraged with messages telling them that a positive mental attitude is the magic potion that will make them successful, dynamic, happy, and rich.

In my opinion, no other selling principle has been more misunderstood or misapplied than this one. The misuse of this principle has, I believe, caused more harm than any other single idea currently in vogue within the sales profession.

This idea has created a generation of salesmen who are *attitude addicts.* These people often seem incapable of the sustained effort it takes to succeed. Many are brainwashed into thinking that a positive mental attitude will guarantee health, wealth, and happiness. That, and most of the other ideas that have grown out of the basic "P.M.A." concept, are worthless garbage. Don't turn me off, now. Read on.

Before I go on any further, let me state up front that I believe in a positive mental attitude, and I practice having one myself. It may seem unusual at first that I'm criticizing a principle that I teach and use. The key issue for me, however, is not the principle itself but *how it is applied.* There are many ingredients necessary for success. A positive mental attitude is only one, and it's less important than many others.

The great danger for many salesmen is that their positive mental attitude has become a liability instead of an asset. The positive mental attitude by itself, unaccompanied by a plan and positive physical action, is worthless.

The mind, like the body, has its own system for warning us when something is wrong. Fear, worry, and concern are to the mind what the pain response is to the body. Pain communicates a message that action is needed to correct a physical problem. If you take pain-killers to mask that pain, the problem could become much worse. It might even kill you. In the same way, fear, worry, and concern exist to warn you that you need to take action to improve a bad situation.

I may be just an ol' country boy, and I don't have a Ph.D. in psychology, but I *do* know this: If you're broke, in debt, job hopping, or having trouble at home, you should *not* feel good about it! You should be concerned, fearful, and worried. Those emotions are telling you something. They're telling you to *take action* and do something to improve the situation before it's too late.

If you psych yourself up with your positive mental attitude, it can have an effect on your mind similar to the effect of pain-killers on your body. When you artificially convince yourself that everything is great when it really isn't, it can delay you from doing what needs to be done to *really* make things great. Instead of "feeling good," you need to dig down, suck up your gut, and get your butt in gear—you have to *do* something!

I'm all for having a positive mental attitude, but I'm very much against substituting that attitude for planning, preparation, and hard work. I don't believe that any positive attitude can call up these necessary elements to successful salesmanship.

I was recently at a sales convention with a good friend of mine, Kozell Boren. Kozy, as he likes to be called, is the manufacturing and marketing genius behind Gulf Industries. As we talked, a young salesman asked Kozy how he kept himself motivated. The young man asked, "How do you keep up the pace without getting into a slump?" Without hesitation, Kozy said, "I have enough character to get up and do the things that need to be done." This is a simple and profound statement that all salespeople should hear. Do something. Do what needs to be done. Above all, take ACTION.

Hiring and training new salespeople is a part of my job. Often, I deal with new hires who are in difficult and sometimes desperate situations. I've trained people who have no money, no car, no home and, worst of all, no hope. I empathize with desperate people, especially since I was desperate once myself, and I can remember exactly what it's like. I have, however, never met anyone who couldn't do something to improve their situation.

People need to be taught the importance of working hard and taking action. A positive mental attitude by itself is never enough. If you substitute a positive mental attitude for hard work and planning, it will cause failure.

When I review job applications, I notice that people who change jobs frequently, jumping from one opportunity to another, also tend to be those who are preoccupied with the concept of the positive mental attitude. These salespeople have become so enamored with wishful thinking that they've become incapable of exerting the sustained effort it takes to succeed.

If a person who's in a desperate situation wants real relief, he or she needs to take the initiative, use some imagination, and get busy. He or she will develop a positive mental attitude as the *result* of this initiative.

I've found over the years that a positive mental attitude is not as likely to produce positive physical action as positive physical action is to produce a positive mental attitude. Imagine two salesmen…one has a great attitude and no plan, and the other has a poor attitude, but a good plan and a lot of action. Guess which of these two is more likely to succeed! You should never just sit there and dream of winning big in the lottery. Go out and buy a ticket! *Then* you can dream about winning big!

I've interviewed many prospective salespeople over the years, and have seen one familiar pattern over and over again. When I talk about a positive mental attitude and setting high goals, most people get very excited. Then, when I tell them about how much study and hard work it'll take to reach those goals, I lose about half of them. Later, when I insist they start in on that hard work,

I lose another half of those remaining. For those "attitude junkies," the traditional American work ethic has all but disappeared.

As professional salespeople, it is up to every one of us to regain and use that work ethic. A seven-point formula that will help ensure success in any endeavor is:

1. *DECIDE* what you want to achieve.
2. *PLAN* how you are going to achieve it.
3. *WORK* as hard as you must to achieve your goals.
4. *STUDY* to learn everything you need to know.
5. *PREPARE* yourself to succeed in every way possible.
6. *DON'T QUIT* until you've reached your goals.
7. *TAKE THESE STEPS* with a positive mental attitude, optimistically expecting to succeed.

A positive mental attitude that is unaccompanied by a plan and action inevitably leads to frustration and disillusionment. Action is the mark of a leader and a winner. Think of the Positive Mental Attitude concept as a great guy, but always remember that he's Physical Action's skinny little red-headed brother. Take both of them to work with you, if you can, but by all means take Big Brother.

SUMMARY: "SUCCESS COMES FROM A POSITIVE MENTAL ATTITUDE"

A. There is a proper time to experience every emotion.
B. There is a proper emotional, mental, and physical response for every situation.
C. Our emotions prepare us to take the appropriate actions to deal with our situation.

Example: Fear prepares us to deal with danger. When we are in danger, fear organizes our mental and physical resources for fight or flight.

Likewise, when things are not going well on the job, in the home, or in any other area of endeavor, your situation will evoke the proper emotional, mental, and physical response.

To artificially inject a feeling of euphoria when your situation is
   desperate is harmful. Your mind and body are deprived of the
   proper stimulation to galvanize them into the proper action.
It is just as harmful to be overly euphoric and optimistic when
   your situation is bad as it is to be depressed when your situation is good.
When things need changing, the most appropriate emotion is
   grim determination that will evoke the proper action.
A positive mental attitude has become the opiate of the masses
   of salespeople. Don't let it be yours. Take action!

MYTH 4: "SETTING HIGH GOALS"

A lot of sales literature has been written in recent years about
the importance of setting high goals. The popular cliché is
"Shoot for the sun…you may not hit it, but you'll probably hit
the moon." Another version goes something like this: "What the
mind of man can conceive, man can achieve." Sound good,
don't they? Well, they're dead wrong. The idea of setting objectives that you probably won't achieve goes hand in hand with
the popular misconceptions about a positive mental attitude.

Some time ago I took part in a sales seminar. Everyone in
attendance was asked to write down extremely high sales goals
for the year. Needless to say, everyone in the room had declared
himself a millionaire within minutes. What's the harm? you may
think. Why not set high goals so that you can imagine and strive
for results that you might not otherwise even consider? Well, the
answer is that it simply doesn't work. In fact, setting goals that
you can't achieve will lead you to accomplish *less* than you would
have achieved without them.

The basic problem with this idea focuses on how we learn and
how our habits are formed. As you know, most of the things we
do are hardest the first time we attempt them. They then become easier as we do them again and again. After a while, these
repeated acts become habitual.

In this context, setting goals that you never achieve gets you *accustomed* to failure. The truth is, if you shoot for the sun and miss, you won't hit the moon—you'll probably just fly off into empty space. If you visualize yourself as a millionaire without a plan to become one or a commitment to the preparation and hard work needed to accomplish that goal, you'll achieve nothing. Since you usually become good at what you do frequently, it doesn't make any sense to become good at failing. When you set your goals, think them through carefully. Never set one that you don't have a carefully worked out plan to achieve, and make sure you're willing to work hard enough to accomplish the goals you set.

Whenever you set a goal for yourself that you don't achieve, it should absolutely tear you up. You should make failing feel so unpleasant that you'll never want to do it again. The best way to progress toward ultimate success is to move steadily from victory to victory. When you set realistic, achievable goals, you'll get used to winning—winning will become something you'll *expect* to do. Then, you should set even higher goals, and set out to achieve *them.*

Setting goals should be a lot like planning a vacation trip. You start by deciding where you want to go. Then you plan how you're going to get there, and when you plan to arrive. Once these goals are set, you do what you need to do to get where you want to go when you want to be there. Your sales goals should be no different. Once a goal is set, it should be unacceptable for you *not* to make it. Dream and plan, then work. That's the only way to make your goals become your accomplishments.

SUMMARY: "SETTING HIGH GOALS"

The goals you set are a promise you make to yourself.

Having made a promise, especially a promise to yourself, make sure you keep it.

Never make an unrealistic promise you can't keep.

Setting goals that you do not make is practicing failure.

Success comes from setting a goal, making it, then setting and making higher goals.

MYTH 5: "GREAT SALESPEOPLE ARE BORN, NOT MADE"

You must have heard about him at some point...the natural born salesman. He has the gift of gab. He makes friends easily. He makes sales by using natural wit and charm. His instincts are a natural part of his personality. Just as great singers are born with natural vocal talent, the born salesman is born with the ability to turn even the toughest prospects into sold customers. He sounds perfect...too good to be true. And, like most things that sound too good to be true, he is. The "born salesman," as described by those who believe in him, doesn't exist.

Probably the most debilitating speech impairment any salesperson can have is the "gift of gab." This gift, often assumed to be a great asset, can become his or her greatest liability. Think of a boxer who has a devastating left hook. He may come to rely on this single skill to win fights instead of developing his stamina, footwork combinations, and self-discipline. The asset has become a liability. This type of boxer will never be a champion.

Like the boxer, a salesperson who relies on his personality, his wit, and his glib tongue often neglects to study the principles of salesmanship. He may also develop poor work habits. Salesmen like that will never be more than peddlers. They'll probably be frustrated by their lack of professional advancement, and bounce from one job to the next without ever understanding why they continue to fail.

As I interview prospective salespeople, I sometimes encounter individuals whose personal charm and magnetism would excite any sales manager. Soon, however, I discover the sad fact that this is another "natural born salesman." This individual has always relied on his charm to win big opportunities, but he's never made a commitment to the hard work, study, and self-discipline that it takes to succeed. He just doesn't have what it takes. Soon, he'll be off to pursue some new opportunity where he can be a celebrity for a little while. Sadly, this person's natural talent ends up holding him back from success.

If you want to be a good salesman, you've got a lot to learn. To be a *master* salesman, you have to make the same kind of commitment that anyone pursuing a degree in law, music, or medicine must make. Salespeople must understand many aspects of human psychology and salesmanship. They must understand motivation, marketing, advertising, and many other related subjects. They must also have an intimate knowledge of the product or service they're selling.

In one sense, salesmanship is much like the game of golf. Millions may play the game, but only a few ever pay the price to become professionals. In the game of sales, don't be a duffer—be a pro! In the long run, you're as likely to become a great salesman without hard work and study as you are to become a brain surgeon without studying medicine and sophisticated surgical techniques.

How would you like to be operated on by a doctor who said, "Oh, I have not studied medicine. I have not practiced medicine. I just think I am a natural born doctor." That makes as much sense as someone thinking that personality and a glib tongue makes him a salesman.

Another common idea that accompanies the "born salesman" myth states that a good salesperson is unorganized and spontaneous. In fact, an impromptu salesperson is never very good. After all, good salespeople are *great* actors. Just as all great actors make every performance *look* spontaneous and unrehearsed, they never are. Excellent stage performances are developed over a period of time, starting with a script that must be studied carefully, followed by rehearsal after rehearsal until every element of the performance is perfected and polished. Dance routines are choreographed and drilled until perfect precision seems effortless. Like these stage performers, every great salesperson must be scripted, rehearsed, and choreographed to the most minute detail.

Think about the other professionals with whom you deal. Doctors typically study for twenty-one years before they can practice their profession, lawyers train for about nineteen years, and neither usually earns anything while he or she studies. For some reason that I've never understood, many salespeople who think of themselves as sales professionals are not willing to *prepare* themselves to succeed as these other professionals do...despite the fact that they can "earn while they learn!"

Customers want and deserve to do business with a well-prepared professional salesperson. You deserve the opportunity to succeed that only preparation and hard work will give you.

Our profession offers more opportunity, more excitement, and more advantages than any other. It's logical, then, that we should be willing to pay a price for success. That price is the preparation and practice that will give us the winning edge with our customers. A good salesperson's words, gestures, and actions should always be perfectly synchronized. Everything should be practiced until the total presentation is smooth, spontaneous, and polished. Only then can a truly effective salesperson project the confidence, skill, and professionalism that define success in sales.

SUMMARY: "GREAT SALESPEOPLE ARE BORN, NOT MADE"

Being a professional salesperson, like being a professional in any other occupation, requires study, practice, and hard work.

Having natural talent often causes failure because it causes us not to recognize the importance of study, practice, and hard work.

Success frequently does not come to salespeople with natural talent.

Success comes to salespeople who perfect their talent through study, practice, and hard work.

MYTH 6: "YOU'VE GOT TO QUALIFY THE CUSTOMER"

Recently, one of my sales managers suffered a severe slump in his business. When I looked into it, I discovered that he'd been to a sales seminar, and had been applying the sales technique he'd learned there. This technique called for the salesperson to qualify the customer at various points during the presentation to see if he or she was really interested. This was done by asking questions starting early in the presentation. These questions would run along the lines of "Mr. Customer, if I can get my price in line with your budget, are you prepared to make a purchase today?" As the presentation progressed, more questions were asked to get more and more commitment from the customer.

Now, use some common sense and think about this approach for a minute. Can any customer hearing that question early in the presentation know if he or she will be ready to make a purchase at its conclusion? Of course not! The customer doesn't yet have enough information to make an intelligent decision.

First, the customer doesn't know what the price will be. Second, the customer doesn't yet know what the features of the product or service are. Third, and most important of all, the customer doesn't yet know how he or she is going to *feel* about the product or service because you haven't had the opportunity to *build value*.

Sales presentations are often made to customers who've said, "I'll look, but I probably won't buy." If this customer is forced or tricked into saying "yes" to some minor point, he is also forced to say or at least think about reasons why he should also be saying "no" to protect his own position. Frequently, the customer will keep these reasons to himself until the end of the presentation. At that point, they come out as one final and irreversible "no," and the sale is lost. This is why the *only* qualifying you ever should do is to make sure that the person to whom you're talking is the person with the authority to make the buying decision.

The two key points to keep in mind about this issue are:

1. The customer shouldn't have to make any decisions until he or she knows all of the facts, including the price. Until you reach that point, it's neither wise nor fair for you to expect the customer to make any decision.

2. The customer shouldn't be given the price until you have built so much value in your product that he or she is ready to say yes. Until the customer has been sold on the

value of your product or service, he or she can't know what the decision will be at any price.

The truly professional salesperson allows his or her customers to remain uncommitted until they have the facts and are ready to say yes. When you ask leading questions to "qualify" your customers, you're being unfair both to the customer and to yourself. You're unfair to the customer because you want him to make a commitment before he has the information he needs to make an informed decision. You're being unfair to yourself because every qualifying question you ask provides the customer with another chance, and perhaps another reason, to say no.

SUMMARY: "YOU'VE GOT TO QUALIFY THE CUSTOMER"

Qualifying the customer to see if he will buy before you are ready to close the sale is counterproductive.

The customer does not know how he will feel about your product or service until you have made him experience owning it.

It is not fair to ask the customer to make any decisions before he has all the facts.

If you force the customer to agree with you before he is ready to buy, you also force him to reaffirm mentally or verbally the reasons he should not buy to protect his own position.

MYTH 7: "NEVER CALL ON A CUSTOMER WHEN HE OR SHE IS BUSY"

The sales gurus who sell this idea have obviously never paid much attention to some basic truths about human nature. Often, salespeople who buy into this myth will make the mistake of trying to isolate their business prospects in a back room or office away from the distractions of the business. These salespeople apparently don't want their important presentation to be interrupted by having their customer see *his* customers buying products and spending their money.

The most difficult time for any independent businessman is

when the cash register is not ringing. On the other hand, when that same businessman is busy, handling lots of customers and making sales hand over fist, he naturally feels prosperous. You don't have to be a psychologist to understand that anyone who has a lot of money in his pocket is more likely to buy than someone whose pockets are empty.

The Bible tells a story about a man who wanted to get some bread from his neighbor. The Bible says the neighbor gave the man the bread *because* he came at an inconvenient time. If *you* want to make some bread, catch your customers at an inconvenient time—when they are busy.

This leads to another even more crucial angle on the same point. We all feel that our schedules are important. We all make a prioritized list of the things we need to do in our days. When someone succeeds in interrupting our important schedule, we generally place more importance on the interruption than we would if we didn't have anything else to do at the moment. This can directly translate to a greater value being placed subconsciously on your product or service; if it was important enough to break the customer's valuable schedule for, it very well may be worth buying.

You should master the delivery of your presentation so completely, and make it so interesting, that people will never be too busy to stop and watch you. My experiences over the years have taught me that the very best time to sell a businessman anything is when he's busy. And the best place to sell that businessman anything is in his place of business, where he can watch his customers spending their money.

SUMMARY: "NEVER CALL ON A CUSTOMER WHEN HE OR SHE IS BUSY"

The best time to sell anything to anyone is when they are feeling prosperous. *Try* to catch your customers when they are busy being paid by *their* customers.

We will interrupt our schedule when something more important than our schedule needs to be dealt with.

The more important the matter that needs to be dealt with, the more justification there is for interrupting our schedule.

Just so, when our schedule is being interrupted we place more importance on the thing that is causing the interruption.

If you interrupt your customer's important schedule to show him your product or service, it puts a high psychological premium on the value of your product or service.

MYTH 8: "SELL YOURSELF BEFORE YOU SELL YOUR PRODUCT"

How many times have you heard this old chestnut? It's a line that always irritates me. The phrase "sell yourself" carries with it a connotation of accommodation and compromise. The basic idea behind this premise is that if you please the customer, he or she will be more likely to buy from you. In fact, just the opposite is true. Salespeople who constantly worry about selling themselves to customers usually sell little else.

On the other hand, salespeople who set high standards and insist on doing things their way are usually high-volume producers. I've never wanted any prospect to buy something from me because he liked me or because I was willing to accommodate him. I want my customers to want my product so badly that they'll buy it without any compromises on my part.

Even if you don't feel that way, and are willing to compromise your own personality to make a sale, I don't believe the tactic works. Think about this logically for a moment. Suppose you want to buy a vintage 1968 Mustang. You figure you'll need to spend about three thousand dollars to get one. A man down the street owns just the car you're looking for. It's in mint condition, with low mileage. You find out that he wants to sell the car, and is asking fifteen hundred dollars. The only problem is that you really don't like this guy at all.

Your good buddy also has a '68 Mustang for sale, but it's a wreck that looks as though it's been driven around the world three or four times. It burns oil and belches smoke like a small brush fire. Your friend is asking five thousand dollars for this heap. "It's a collector's item," he says. Now...would you buy the second car just because you like the guy? Of course you wouldn't. What you really want is the right car at the right price.

The only reason people buy anything is the *value* they perceive in the product or service they're considering. If you build enough value in your product or service, you can sell anything. Salespeople who waste time selling themselves typically make washed-out, generic sales presentations that are without vigor and devoid of personality. That kind of salesperson is never likely to impress anyone because he or she is so fearful of offending the prospective buyer.

Selling yourself is an insult to you, because *you* should not be for sale. Your products or services are. Selling yourself is also an insult to your customer. It implies that you believe a customer can be easily swayed by simple, and ultimately meaningless, accommodations.

The process of "selling yourself" diminishes a salesman's pride in who he is and what he does. Great salesmen sell their products or services with great pride. They never compromise their own personality or individuality to please a customer. By always being themselves, they maintain their own self-esteem. They also show their respect for the customer by being straightforward and honest throughout their presentation. It's no big secret, really. Be yourself. Take pride in who you are, and let that pride show through and work for you.

SUMMARY: "SELL YOURSELF BEFORE YOU SELL YOUR PRODUCT"

The customer wants to do business with a professional who takes pride in his or her work. Selling yourself implies accommodation and compromising your own individuality, and is not likely to impress anyone in the long run.

Preserve your own individuality by conducting yourself with pride, self-confidence, and professionalism.

**Sell your product or service with pride, confidence, and profes-
sionalism.**

**Make the customer want your product or service so badly that
they feel compelled to accommodate you.**

**Remember that people won't buy because they like *you*; they will
buy because they *like what you're selling*.**

MYTH 9: "NEVER TELL THE CUSTOMER YOU ARE AN EXPERT"

I have to smile a little whenever I hear someone suggest this
as a way to succeed in sales. It never fails to make me think about
the hundreds of sales I've closed and the tens of thousands of
commission dollars I've earned by making sure my customers
clearly knew that I *am* the expert!

When you're in the sign business, you get a lot of input from
customers. They'll offer any number of ideas. Suggestions I've
heard range from doing the background in a favorite color to
putting a picture of the family cat in a prominent position on
the sign. I'm sure salespeople of all kinds get suggestions also.
Now, many salespeople would tell you that they'd have a better
chance of making the sale if they accommodated these requests.
Wouldn't it make sense, they reason, to give the customer what
he or she wants?

Well, no. What qualifications do these customers have to
make important decisions like this? What experience do they
have in the design of exterior signage or the sale or application
of your product or service? How can they be sure that they've
done the right thing? If you, as a salesperson, are willing to do
anything the customer wants, he or she implicitly learns that you
don't know what is best for that customer or, even worse, that
you don't care about what is best so long as you make the sale.

When asked to accommodate a customer during a presentation, I've often said, "Mr. Customer, if you want to learn how to
play golf, you should ask Arnold Palmer. If you want to learn
how to cook chicken, you should ask Colonel Sanders. But if you

want to know about signs, ask me—I'm the expert!" If the customer resists that idea, I might add a statement like "I really want to do business with you, but I also want to do a professional job. I guess if I can't do it right, it'd be better for both of us if we didn't do it." By the way, I honestly feel that way and I have discovered honesty always pays off.

The truth is, everyone wants to do business with an expert. People want to do business with someone who's absolutely sure of what he or she is doing, and who knows what's best for the customer. The best qualification for any salesperson is his or her self-confidence. I've *often* explained to customers that I was the sign expert, and that if they didn't want to do things the right way, I didn't want to do business. I've never once lost a sale when I've made that kind of statement. Think about this for a moment.

Everyone agrees that customers should be made to feel important when they interact with a salesperson. It makes sense, then, that your customers will feel more important if they're treated with special respect by someone who is an expert in the field. Similarly, they're much less impressed when they're treated well by someone they themselves don't respect. The lesson here is simple: The more important you make yourself, the more important you can make your customer feel. And in reality, you *are* important, because you probably know more about your product or service than they will *ever* know.

SUMMARY: "NEVER TELL THE CUSTOMER YOU ARE AN EXPERT"

Everyone wants to do business with an expert.

Your customer is usually not sure that buying your product or service is the correct thing to do.

The most effective thing you can do is assure your customer that you are the expert and that you know what is best. Do the work you need to do to insure that this is in fact the case.

Your customer wants, needs, and deserves to know that he or she is doing business with an expert.

MYTH 10: "WHEN THE CUSTOMER SHOWS BUYING SIGNS, CLOSE"

A speaker at a recent sales seminar made this statement with such conviction and showy fanfare that over two hundred salespeople accepted it as gospel truth. At first glance, the idea *does* seem logical. However, what we have here is another one of those concepts that become absurd when they're analyzed closely.

Does it make any sense to close a sale before a customer fully understands the benefits, responsibilities, liabilities, and ramifications of the sale? Wouldn't that increase the possibility of dissatisfied customers who are angry with you because you didn't give them all the facts? Closing at the earliest possible opportunity is as silly as telling a duck hunter to shoot the moment he hears a quack.

There is, of course, an appropriate time to close a sale. You, as a salesperson, must choose the time and place to close the sale for the best results. That time is: (1) when the customer knows everything he needs to know in order to make an intelligent decision, and (2) when the customer is ready to say yes.

A salesman has not earned his commission when he's told his customers about a product or a service. A salesman has not earned his commission when he has caused his customer to want his product or service. A salesman *has* earned his commission only when he's made the customer *understand* all the facts about the product or service. We've done our job as salespeople well when we can be sure that our customer has purchased something that will provide complete satisfaction.

SUMMARY: "WHEN THE CUSTOMER SHOWS BUYING SIGNS, CLOSE"

The proper time to close the sale is when two things happen:

1. The customer has all the information he needs to make an intelligent decision.

2. The customer is ready to say yes.

Trying to close the sale when the customer shows buying signs turns out the way other things you do prematurely turn out. It leads to frustration and disappointment.

MYTH 11: "SELLING IS A NUMBERS GAME"

Many variations of this idea are taught and discussed throughout the sales community. "Selling is a numbers game," they tell us. "X number of calls will result in Y number of sales." Many of the salespeople I've trained over the years have expressed their own versions of this little axiom. Like the other myths we've considered here, I consider this one to be silly, unfounded, and potentially self-defeating.

I've often heard people say, "Well, we've gotten all the 'nos' out of the way...now we can get in there and sell one!" Another variation of this idea goes something like this: "We usually sell one out of fifteen calls, and we've made ten calls, so we're only five calls away from a sale!" Again, think about how absurd this idea really is.

If you're not doing your presentation correctly...if you are not building enough value...if you don't know how to close the sale...you're no closer to making a sale after ten calls than you were before the first. Can you apply this practice to anything else?

Imagine you're playing golf and your shots are constantly hooking into the woods. Would the appropriate solution be to hit more shots and watch them all hook consistently into the woods? Of course not. You must correct the positions of your wrists and feet. You have to identify the problem, correct it, and *then* take your next shot. Only after you make the necessary corrections will your shot head off in the right direction. Make the necessary corrections in your sales presentation, and your very next call should result in a sale.

I firmly believe in the value and importance of hard work, but I also believe in working smart. *Every* presentation should conclude with a sale. If it doesn't, you've somehow failed. Hundreds of salespeople have watched me sell. Some have seen me fail to make a sale. No one, however, has ever heard me offer an excuse for not making a sale, except "I just didn't do it right." I'd failed to do it right that time, but I also promised that I'd do it better the next time. I have never allowed myself to justify, minimize, or get used to failing.

If you handle your presentation improperly, if you don't understand the principles of selling, or if you apply those principles incorrectly, the "numbers game" won't add up for you. If you apply correct selling principles and work hard, you'll get rich in direct sales.

SUMMARY: "SELLING IS A NUMBERS GAME"

Selling, like every other skill, requires practice.

If you do not make calls, if you do not make your presentation regularly, you will not acquire the skills to become successful.

Practicing your presentation incorrectly, however, is just as harmful as not practicing it at all.

If you are selling one out of ten calls and want to improve production, you should do two things:

> **First, improve your sales technique until you can sell two or three out of ten calls.**

> **Second, make more calls.**

To become successful at selling, you must analyze your presentation, eliminate your mistakes, and practice your successes.

MYTH 12: "ASK LEADING QUESTIONS"

This popular principle proposes that if you ask your customer questions that have only one logical answer, you can maneuver the conversation where you want it to go. Another version of this idea states that if you get the customer to agree with you on small points, he'll be more likely to agree with you when you ask for the order. Many of the same principles apply here that apply to qualifying the customer.

A basic problem with this "rule" is that it violates a much older rule—the Golden Rule. The Golden Rule states that we should treat people in the same way that we want to be treated. I like straight talk, don't you? Well, I think our customers feel exactly the same way. If you apply a little common sense here, you can readily see just how harmful the practice of "asking leading questions" can be. Actually, in general you can get a feel for whether a sales tactic is effective or counterproductive by just putting yourself in the place of the customer.

Consider these points: If someone tries to get you to say something you don't want to say by asking leading questions, don't you *recognize* what they're doing? When you realize what's being done to you, don't you *resent* it? Don't you then become *evasive*? Now, given this scenario, imagine a customer in the same situation. Aren't evasiveness and resentment the very *last* feelings you want to evoke from your customers?

Remember that our customers are generally as smart as we are. They don't like to be manipulated any more than we do. Like just about everyone else, customers prefer straight talk, not word games and manipulation.

Consider this example of a similar tactic now being taught to hundreds of salespeople, and think about how *you* would react if it were used on you. Imagine that you're in a clothing store looking for a new shirt or blouse. You find one that you like, and you ask a clerk if it is available in red. The clerk then asks you, "If we have it in red, will you buy it?" Wouldn't that approach make you angry? Why, you would ask yourself, should I have to commit myself to making a purchase just to see how it looks in red? How can I know if I'll even *like* it until I see it? As you can see, this kind of tactic not only doesn't work, but it can actually make a salesperson less effective. Experience has shown me that this approach might sell books or audiocassettes to gullible salespeople, but it will sell little else.

Asking a customer for any kind of commitment before the selling process is complete is ultimately futile. When customers consider the purchase of something that's very important to them—an item or service that appeals to their ego and their sense of self—that decision-making process can be compared, quite literally, to the process of childbirth.

A woman does not know exactly how she will feel about her child, and what sacrifices she will be willing to make for that child, until the child is born. As she holds the child a bond forms that she could never have imagined previously.

Similarly, your customers can't know how they'll feel about your product or service, or the sacrifices they'll be willing to make in order to own it, until *you* cause them to feel or experience the benefits your product or service offers. As your customers become more and more familiar with your product or service, they'll form a personal bond with it. They can only truthfully answer their own questions about the product or service when the entire process is completed, and the bond is completely formed.

SUMMARY: "ASK LEADING QUESTIONS"

Asking leading questions is a form of manipulation. Don't manipulate your customer; educate your customer.

Asking leading questions is an insult. Don't insult your customer; edify your customer.

Asking leading questions evokes resentment, distrust, and evasiveness. Evoke good will, trust, and confidence by talking straight.

Only when your customer "knows" your product or service will he or she be able to make a commitment to it.

MYTH 13: "YOU LEARN FROM YOUR MISTAKES"

Here we have another little gem of wisdom that we often hear in everyday conversation. Again, this phrase is somewhat misdirected. A mistake may cause you not to make that same mistake a second time, but it will teach you little else. For example, if you use Compound W instead of Preparation H, you probably would never make that mistake again, but you might use Bonocca instead of Visine. There are, after all, an endless number of other mistakes out there. You'll never run out of new mistakes to make. From this standpoint, you can see that you don't gain very much by avoiding the repetition of a single error.

Mistakes don't teach...but successes do. You learn most effectively by discovering how to do something well, then improving on what you've learned. Salespeople, as a rule, tend to look for new ideas and new approaches to selling. They look for the "magic bullet" that will make selling easy. In fact, selling only becomes easy when you learn its fundamental principles and continually build, practice, and improve on them.

Success doesn't depend on being at the right place at the right time. Success doesn't depend on the number of opportunities that life offers you. Instead, success depends on your ability and willingness to seize your opportunities and take advantage of them. When you discover that something is working, develop it...explore it...exploit it...and master it. This is the true path to success.

SUMMARY: "YOU LEARN FROM YOUR MISTAKES"

You do not learn from your mistakes. You learn by eliminating your mistakes and improving on your successes.

Don't waste time overanalyzing mistakes. Analyze success.

Don't dwell on mistakes. Dwell on success.

Avoid making mistakes and by all means avoid repeating mistakes.

Progress comes from analyzing, exploring, exploiting, and repeating successes.

MYTH 14: "CRITICIZE THE FAULT, NOT THE PERSON"

If you've ever taken on the responsibilities of hiring, managing, or training a sales force, you know that it's a job fraught with frustration. A large percentage of newly hired salespeople have personal problems that have to be overcome. Often, they lack such basics as a car, money, or training. More importantly, many lack the self-discipline necessary to come to meetings on time, or to learn the skills they have to master before they can become successful.

The idea that we should "criticize the fault, not the person" has a certain attraction to it. It appeals to our basic sense of mercy and forgiveness. When you look at it closely, however, you realize that it can mislead and harm people who need direction in their lives by relieving them of responsibility for their actions.

An unwillingness to take responsibility for one's actions is at the heart of all ineffectiveness and failure. Show me a person who is always late, unprepared, broke, and generally undisciplined, and I'll show you a person who has an excuse for everything that goes wrong. If you're a manager who's willing to criticize the fault instead of placing the blame where it belongs—on the salesperson—you are only reinforcing the bad habits that will ultimately lead that person to failure. Managers have to talk straight with their salespeople, just as salespeople must talk straight with their customers.

Let's get to the heart of the issue. Being late for appointments, being broke, writing checks that bounce, not knowing a sales presentation, and all the other traits that accompany professional failure are *not* random events that "just happen." Failure is not just the result of bad luck. It is generally caused by a flaw in your character. When people take responsibility for their actions and own up to their responsibilities, they've taken the first step toward correcting their problems.

SUMMARY: "CRITICIZE THE FAULT, NOT THE PERSON"

The first step towards becoming responsible is to take responsibility for your own actions.

The first step towards teaching someone to become successful is to teach them to take responsibility for their own actions.

If you are serious about helping someone overcome their faults, talk straight. Tell them about their faults and the consequences of repeating their faults. Tell them about their good habits and the rewards associated with continuing their good habits. Encourage them to eliminate their faults and improve on their good habits.

CHAPTER 3

Starting a Career in Sales

If you're just starting a career in sales, or if you're in sales and not doing as well as you'd like to, you need to get your career on the right track. You should have many exciting opportunities ahead of you. If you work hard and apply the appropriate sales principles, you can look forward to a fulfilling professional career and substantial financial reward. These opportunities aren't limited to any particular group of people or personality types. In this section, I'll explore the variety of highly paid opportunities that sales offers to all types of people.

As I've noted earlier, I firmly believe that direct sales provides people with the best opportunity to earn significant income in the shortest period of time when compared to any other profession. Opportunities in sales are available to everyone regardless of age, sex, religion, or race. Sales affords freedoms that most other careers deny. Very often this profession offers opportunities to have your own business with no up-front investment. When you apply yourself, you can advance rapidly. This fact makes it possible for those making mid-life career changes to have a second chance to start over and still make it to the top.

What follows are some important points that anyone considering a sales career should keep in mind:

1. First, check out any opportunities closely. Never risk

your future or the future of your family by involving yourself in some ill-conceived scam. Many good and legitimate opportunities are available in sales today, but beware…there are parasites out there who make their livings by taking advantage of unwary salespeople!

2. Once you've selected the opportunity that's right for you, make the commitment necessary to succeed at it. Many would-be salespeople become frustrated when they don't become "superstars" immediately. They move from job to job, never sticking with one long enough to make it pay off. It takes time, effort, and commitment to succeed at anything worthwhile.

3. Be sure to involve your family as you develop your new career. If you're to succeed in sales, you must have your family's cooperation. There's much for you to learn at the beginning, and there will be times when your earnings will be low. Be sure not to make unrealistic promises or commitments to your family. Salespeople who make that mistake only put undue pressure on themselves at a time when they can least cope with it. Be realistic, be open, and make your success a team effort that'll keep you moving forward even when the going gets tough.

4. Now, get to work! Get your tail in gear and work until you've succeeded. Never miss or be late for a meeting. Don't try to get by with the minimum amount of preparation; master the task and expect to work hard.

Let me interject a personal note here on what "work" really means. Because I've been so successful in sales, I've developed a reputation as a very lucky man. Since I'm also something of a showman, I do whatever I can to perpetuate this myth. Well, the truth is, luck has had nothing to do with my success. Let me be honest and tell you about what *really* made the difference for me.

When I first went to work for Gulf Sign Company, I assigned myself a foreman, and gave him absolute control over me. MY FOREMAN WAS MY SCHEDULE. That foreman told me that I had to start working at eight o'clock in the morning and sell at least one sign or make five presentations a day, six days a week, every week. My foreman told me that if I didn't make a sale one day, I couldn't eat, rest, or sleep on the following day until I made a sale.

My foreman didn't change his mind if it was raining or snowing. He didn't care if I'd earned two thousand dollars the previous day. He relentlessly urged me on day by day, week by week. On some days it was easy to sell. It seemed as though everyone wanted to buy. On other days, it was difficult and frustrating. I'd find myself working all day and most of the night with no sale. On some occasions, I'd make sales calls at three or four o'clock in the morning, having worked continuously since the start of the previous day. I can remember at least three occasions on which I came home too tired to undress. I dropped my briefcase as I walked in the door and fell onto my bed with my clothes and shoes still on…but I had an order in my pocket!

Along with my commitment to hard work, I also continuously practiced, prepared, and studied. I worked on my presentation, practicing it over and over again. I also analyzed and researched every aspect of the sign business. I studied the history of signs from ancient times to the present. I studied the construction of signs. When I started selling in a new area, I studied the role signs played in the economical development of that area, and how the area's economy had evolved over the years. I'd never settle for not knowing. I'd find out what I needed to know by looking it up. This commitment to study, preparation, and hard work would make anyone successful at anything they set their mind to.

5. Demonstrate loyalty. So long as you are affiliated with a company, be loyal to it. Often, new salespeople excuse their lack of success by criticizing their job, their boss, or their co-workers. As this barrage of criticism continues, the salesperson's spouse frequently turns against the employer and encourages the salesperson to quit. Soon, these bad feelings spiral into inevitable failure. Salespeople who retain

their loyalty to their employers and place blame for slow sales where it belongs—with themselves—are much more likely to overcome their problems and succeed. These loyal salespeople also often find that the co-workers they initially may dislike become their closest friends! The principle here is a simple one: Give everyone a chance, and stick by your team. Having made a commitment to succeed at this job, quit looking around and concentrate on succeeding. Remember, a double-minded man is unstable in all his ways. Loyalty pays.

6. Spouses should make a sincere effort to understand the difficult situation that any new salesperson is in. That person has a lot to learn, and a lot to do. The pressure to perform is great. The salesperson should be able to relax as much as possible at home. Spouses should never ask their partners if they've sold anything. They don't ever have to—that's the kind of information that salespeople always volunteer freely. When they don't sell, they never want to be reminded of it.

Remember that during the early stages of a career, victories are measured in more ways than just bottom-line sales. New salespeople need assurance that their partners understand and empathize with the challenges they face. Spouses have to remember that salespeople will spend one-third of the rest of their lives on the job. They should never relegate their mates to a job that doesn't satisfy them personally or professionally. Support at home is critical to anyone striving for success in sales.

7. The saying "dress for success" is a cardinal rule for all salespeople. If you're starting in sales or making a change into selling, you must dress appropriately. The best way to learn what to wear is to look at other salespeople. Try to dress better than they do. If you see that your fellow salespeople all wear dress shoes, don't wear cowboy boots. Always dress as well as you can. If you can't afford to buy new shoes, polish your old ones. If you can't buy a new suit, clean and press the one you have. Make sure your hair is cut, well groomed, and professional looking. Remember that selling is enough of a

challenge as it is; none of us need any added handicaps. Be sure to pay close attention to your personal grooming or hygiene.

8. Remember that if your sales opportunity is a good one, it will demand a lot of hard work from you. You have to study your presentation, and learn everything you can about your product or service before you see your first prospect. If you're new to the sales profession, you'll have to work even harder than other salespeople in order to compete effectively. You should be prepared to put in long, difficult hours of hard work before you achieve the success you desire.

ASSETS AND LIABILITIES

Over the years, I've given a lot of thought to why some of the people I hire succeed while others fail. Often, the people everyone expects to work miracles are the ones who don't make it, and vice versa. My experience has shown me that the difference is often how these individuals perceive and manage their personal assets and liabilities.

OLDER SALESPEOPLE

Quite often people start a new sales career relatively late in life. How these people deal with the age issue is often decisive. Sometimes the transition into the new sales position by older people isn't easy. If an older person feels diminished or humbled by a low-level sales assignment, or by working for a young manager, he or she will probably fail.

When older salespeople are asked to do things in a new way, they sometimes resent it, and quickly resume their old, well-established habits. One mistake commonly made by older salespeople is to constantly talk with their customers and co-workers about their previous position or career. They tend to relive their past rather than live for the present and build for the future.

If you're an older person who's moving into a new sales position, consider the following points:

1. As I mentioned earlier, salespeople are actors. Your customers don't know you, and know nothing about your professional status. Good actors can be anything or anybody they want to be. With a little work and practice, you can look and act like the knowledgeable expert you're striving to be. Your customers will take you seriously because you'll convey the serious professionalism of all successful salespeople.

2. Older people are more likely to be trusted than younger people. This is a common truism that can be applied in all areas of life, not just sales. Use this fact to your advantage.

3. Older people are listened to more carefully, and are usually treated with more respect than younger people. Use *that* to your advantage.

4. Life is an adventure, and older people have experienced more of that adventure than their younger co-workers. If you're an older salesperson, think of all the experience you've had as a tremendous asset—an asset that's unique to you, and that can never be taken away. Look at each day and each project you undertake as a new challenge that will add to your body of experience, and no one will be able to compete with you.

5. There is no other profession that offers the same potential for rapid upward mobility that direct sales offers. If you do a good job, if you're reliable, and if you're committed, you'll probably be at the top in a short time. Unlike the standard corporate career path, you won't have to spend years "paying your dues" working in lower echelon positions before advancing to higher levels.

Many older people could have tremendous adventures in direct sales. It's a career that'll allow you to meet new people, see new things, and make as much money as you want. As always, though, it pays to be careful. Remember that there are many so-called sales opportunities out there that really have only one objective—to sell *you* something. Be very wary whenever you're asked to buy a product before you're given a chance to sell it.

VERY YOUNG SALESPEOPLE

If you're very young, you may often find yourself frustrated by prospective customers who don't take you seriously. If you treat your customers with respect, you're considered naïve. If you're too forceful, you're considered a brash "smart aleck." If your frustration causes you to dwell on these apparent liabilities, you may end up providing yourself with excuses to fail. Consider, instead, the following assets available to you:

1. You have boundless energy and the eternal optimism of youth. When you commit yourself to action, you can work circles around other salespeople.

2. You haven't developed the poor work habits that cause many salespeople to fail.

3. You probably haven't developed the other bad habits that so often lead to failure among salespeople. These include drinking, wasting money, wasting time, pre-judging customers, etc.

4. You probably do not yet have heavy financial obligations. This permits you to learn your trade thoroughly and effectively with less pressure to succeed immediately.

5. You probably have more mobility than the average salesperson. You have the freedom to go where your selling skills are needed the most.

6. Most people will excuse outlandish behavior from a young person. This gives you the freedom to try newer and more original sales approaches. The less inhibited you are, the more options you have available to add to your "sales arsenal."

7. When young people display true professionalism, they stand out. People tend to notice them and pay attention to what they have to say.

When young people develop their selling skills, they can rest assured of a secure future. The reason for this is simple. There will *always* be a great demand for competent salespeople. When you prepare yourself well and become one of the best, you can't help but succeed.

WOMEN IN SALES

There was a time when sales was a "males only" business, and today's saleswomen still face some of the negative aspects of being a "novelty." A saleswoman calling on a male prospect will often be given a hearing even if the customer has no intention of buying. The customer gets the "ego boost" of a woman's attention while giving no concern to the fact that she may have a quota to meet, bills to pay, or a family to support.

Many businessmen still refuse to take saleswomen seriously. If she's efficient and businesslike, she's considered cool and aloof. If she's friendly and forthcoming, she risks the misinterpretation of her actions as a personal advance. If women aren't tough as nails, darn smart, and just sweet enough, they'll have a tough time making it in sales. Given these common perceptions what, if any, *advantages* do women have in sales today? The answer is *plenty*! Consider the following points:

1. Women typically have much less difficulty obtaining the time and attention of prospective customers. As a rule they're considered less threatening than men, and are therefore afforded more opportunities to make presentations. This can be a tremendous advantage for a wise saleswoman who uses good judgment.

2. Most male prospects find it more difficult to be impolite, rude, or angry with saleswomen than salesmen.

3. Saleswomen are more likely to be trusted than the average salesman. This can, naturally, make the entire selling process easier.

In recent years, more and more women have been making career changes into sales, and are now discovering the wonderful advantages that this profession offers. In many cases, if women would put the hours and the energy into sales that they put into other jobs, they could double or triple their income and enjoy many more of the benefits that life has to offer.

NEWLY NATURALIZED CITIZENS

People from all over the world still come to the United States seeking a new life and the many opportunities that our society offers. Language barriers and cultural differences often lead these people to accept low-paying jobs that don't let them take advantage of their talents and skills. Our traditions and customs are often hard for these new Americans to understand. Our business practices may also seem strange and illogical to them. Along with these cultural challenges, new citizens also often face another serious problem—they need to make a living starting from the ground up. They must provide for their families immediately, often with no real assets or security to back them up.

Again, new citizens can perceive these circumstances as liabilities working against them, or they can identify the advantage that these circumstances provide. Consider the following:

1. People who don't speak English well have the luxury of speaking very slowly, and repeating themselves until they are understood. This can be a great asset to any salesperson. It allows him or her to make absolutely sure that the customer understands the proposition being offered.

2. A salesperson with limited English skills might understandably not know what a prospective customer means when he says "no," or "that costs too much money," or "I'm too busy right now." He or she can ignore objections and move ahead building value, which is what really makes the sale.

3. All of us are fascinated by people who come from different cultural backgrounds. If you're a member of a royal family, you can be sure that you'll attract more attention in Paris, Kentucky than you will in Paris, France. If you're a cowboy, you'll probably be treated like a celebrity on Man-

hattan Island, even though you're "just folks" on a ranch in Wyoming. Most Americans are sympathetic to new citizens who are working hard to succeed in this country. After all, we're a nation that was built by immigrants. Many customers that a new citizen will meet can remember their grandparents' tales of those early days in this country, and will empathize with the struggles and the commitment that these people are making to build their new lives.

If you are a new citizen, and you're looking for a job that pays well and offers unlimited opportunity, try direct sales. You are likely to be welcomed by your customers, and given opportunities to sell that other salespeople might not ever have.

ETHNIC BACKGROUND OR RACE

This is clearly a sensitive subject—so much so that it might've been easier for me to avoid it completely. However, that wouldn't be fair to the many motivated individuals of varied ethnic backgrounds or races who are considering a sales career. There are many valuable ideas that can help people of many races and nationalities be more successful in sales.

First, let me *assure* you that I live in the real world, and I know that all forms of prejudice still exist. I've seen it in many different forms and in many different circumstances. I have experienced prejudice myself many times. I remember once selling a sign to a woman who constantly called me a "white devil!" I have often been called a "honkey." Yes, prejudice can be found in the marketplace in many different forms. Still, I don't believe that any sale has ever really been lost just because a salesperson belonged to a particular ethnic group. In other words, I firmly believe that race or ethnic origin doesn't have any effect on selling or in the selling process.

Again, people buy products or services because the value of that product or service exceeds the price in the buyer's mind. Customers generally have little real feeling for a salesperson whom they do not know, regardless of sex, race, or other personal characteristics. Besides, a professional salesperson doesn't want or expect any customer to buy a product or service because the customer likes him or her. Finally, people usually get out of life exactly what they put into it. If you expect people to treat you with respect, they probably will. Conversely, if you expect people to discriminate against you, they probably will.

I can best illustrate this point with a brief story about a black salesman I had in New York. This fellow had the unlikely name of Marcelus Twinkel. At the first sign of prejudice he would throw his unique sales approach into gear, and it went something like this: "I'm Marcelus Twinkel...but you can call me chocolate Twinkel," he'd say. "Now, I know you're probably prejudiced, and you probably think you're smarter than I am. I'm going to sell you something, though, because you're going to like what I *got* so bad, you're going to buy it in spite of the fact that you don't like *me*." And you know what? People *loved* him! He had mastered his presentation so well, and was so effective at building the value of his product, that he became one of the best salesmen I've ever met. Most of my New York salesmen sold one sign a day. Marcelus brought in orders like carrots by the bunch.

Minorities often argue that they are the victims of pay discrimination. This can't possibly happen in direct sales, since a minority salesperson is awarded the same commission as everyone else in the field sales staff. And, since most promotions are based on well-defined sales quotas, advancement in the sales profession is also fair. Performance, not background, is the only criterion for advancement.

In direct sales, more than in almost any other professional endeavor, you receive remuneration that matches what you are worth. For many, this is a fantastic opportunity that shouldn't be missed. For some, of course, this is bad news.

ASSETS AND LIABILITIES: STORIES FROM THE TRENCHES

The ideas I've shared earlier in this section didn't just float in on the breeze. I've developed them over the years by observing many different salespeople in action, and making mental notes of how they make use of the various attributes they bring to their sales careers. On the following pages are the stories of some of the people who helped me develop these principles.

These stories will help clarify these issues, and illustrate how people who are committed to their sales careers can make the unique qualities of their character work for them, and carry them toward success.

BOBBY LEE: TAKE ACTION, DO SOMETHING

Bobby Lee was one of those salespeople who would normally be overlooked—or avoided—by most organizations. His favorite activity was playing his guitar and singing songs he'd written. Sometimes it seemed as though he worked only to support this and other worse habits. One day, when I was based in Yonkers, New York, I ran an ad for new salespeople. One of the first calls I received on the morning the ad appeared was from Bobby Lee. He told me he was interested in the job, but he was calling from Baltimore, Maryland—about five hours away from where I was conducting the interviews. He sounded like an interesting prospect to me, so I told him to come over so we could talk further. That's when he said, "I can't just come over...I'm in Baltimore!" I responded, "Get your butt in your car and drive on over here!" He paused for a moment, then said, "I can't do that. My car's in the garage." I smiled to myself, thinking that I would test his mettle a bit. I told him, "Then get your butt into a Greyhound bus and come on over here!"

He did. I hired and trained him. After his first week on the job, he'd made one thousand dollars and was able to pay for the repairs to his car. Since then Bobby Lee and I have done a lot of selling together. We worked so well together that there was virtually no situation that we could not turn into a sale.

Why did I hire Bobby Lee in the first place? When I met him, I wasn't impressed by his clothing, his education, or his personality. I recognized in him the single characteristic that I value the most—determination. He had the spirit of commitment that is necessary to any successful salesperson. He knew what he wanted, took the action that was necessary to get it, and made it work for him. There's a lot that every salesperson can learn from Bobby Lee!

MILT MANNIX: MOVE UP TO SALES

Since I had started out in sales broke, hopeless, and needing another chance, I seem to have a knack for attracting people with similar problems. I've taught former pig farmers, cab drivers, and chronically unemployed people to sell and be successful. As I became more successful, however, I started attracting people with more stable and successful backgrounds. My training classes started to look like a crazy quilt of different personalities. I had ex-drug addicts and preachers, people with million-dollar homes and others who were living at the Y.M.C.A. Every strata of society was represented in these sessions.

When I was hiring in Boston one day, a very wealthy businessman called and asked for an interview. He told me that he was working as a schoolteacher, but I soon learned that he had also owned several businesses, and came from a very rich and prominent family. Milt Mannix was an imposing figure, both physically and mentally. Even if he had been short, squat, and ugly, Milt's intellect, self-confidence, and bearing would command attention...but Milt was six foot four, and a very good-looking man. As we spoke on the telephone, Milt started to ask me a lot of questions. This annoyed me a little since I'm usually the one who asks all the questions. I was in a hurry and became somewhat abrupt. Milt then told me about his extensive education and professional background. I told him I was impressed and to come over to the motel where I was interviewing so we could talk further. "How do I get there?" he said. Well, I decided that I'd answered enough questions from this guy. I snapped back, "Hey, if you're so smart, you should be able to find the motel by yourself," and hung up.

Later, Milt told me that once he figured out where I was, he drove over planning to "kick some a..." Fortunately for me, he didn't. You see, in addition to his many scholastic and business achievements, Milt also has a background in karate. Instead, he was impressed with what he saw and heard, and went to work as a salesman. Milt is now the manager of our Boston office, earning about twenty-five thousand every month.

As Milt's story shows, selling isn't just for those who have no job or who've failed in other careers. Many successful bank presidents, lawyers, corporation owners, and other professionals take the big step up to sales.

BRUCE MANLEY: YOUNG PEOPLE TRY SALES

A few years ago I was invited to Texas by a group of sales managers to give a speech on the topics of hard work, self-discipline, and professionalism. After I made my speech, I was introduced to a number of people, including an unimposing young man named Bruce. As often happens in situations like that, I shook his hand, made a few quick comments, and moved on to the next person. I quickly forgot him.

Soon after I returned to New York, I got a phone call. "Mr. Allard, this is Bruce from Texas. Remember me?" After he refreshed my memory, he got right to his point. "Mr. Allard, I want to come to work for you!"

I'm always pleased when I inspire someone to go to work for me, so I responded, "Great, come by and see me sometime!" I didn't realize just how inspired this fellow was. He said, "How about right now? I'm just down the street."

I invited him up to my home for a talk. When we sat down together, he told me the story of his education and work experience. To put it bluntly, this young man was convinced that he was a failure at age 19. He asked me if I thought he could possibly start over and really learn how to sell.

I firmly believe that anyone who works hard and makes a real effort can succeed in direct sales, so I agreed to help him if he would do exactly what I said. These days, whenever I hear a salesperson make excuses for failure, I think of this young man and the obstacles he faced. When he first started, he had no *money*, no *training*, no *decent clothes*, and no *car*. He made his early sales calls by walking from business to business carrying his sample case in one hand and his briefcase in the other.

Bruce was very young, and had an innocent, boyish look about him. He soon realized that because of his youthful appearance, he was having a hard time getting potential customers to take him seriously. Bruce soon bought himself a car and the same kind of clothing that his older, more experienced co-workers were wearing. He also worked hard to make *himself* such an effective sales professional that he projected a new-found maturity and sophistication.

A short while ago, this same young man who'd sat in my living room and proclaimed himself a failure bought himself a new *Porsche*, a *powerboat*, and a *new home*. Today, he earns more money in one month than most men his age make in a year.

As I watched and listened to Bruce make a fantastic speech in Long Beach recently, tears came to my eyes. This self-confident, successful young man is the epitomy of success through sales.

JUDY MORRISSY: LADIES TRY SALES

O.K., I admit it...when I first started in direct sales, I was a dyed-in-the-wool chauvinist pig, which is wrong, wrong, wrong. I didn't think that women belonged in sales, or in any part of the business world, for that matter. Whenever women would respond to my ad and come in for an interview, I'd make it so tough on them that they'd soon get the message and go away. I'm ashamed to say that I often said, "Women do well in two places, and neither of those places is sales."

One day in Pittsburgh, a young woman came to see me. This wasn't a typical visitor by any stretch of the imagination. Judy was a college professor with a doctorate in psychology. Someone had told her about my sales philosophy, and she wanted to hear more about my ideas.

After we talked, I had her sit in on a training session with some of my new recruits. I told the others that I'd just hired her, and that she'd start her training right away. Some of the guys looked at me warily, but soon settled into our training routine. I was motivating them, giving them hell, getting them excited, and generally having a good time. Judy sat there in silence, just observing.

Finally, I turned to Judy, the only woman in the room. As I looked at her, I remembered the line that Art Murphy had stung me with so long ago. "Honey," I said, "in sales, you would have two chances to succeed—slim and none. And I think slim just left." Judy looked straight into my eyes and smiled. "Mr. Allard," she said quietly, "you are full of crap!" I said, "Well, that sounds like a challenge." Judy said, "It is. I can do anything any man can do, only better." After the session, I offered Judy a job, and she accepted it.

Judy quit her teaching position at the college to devote all of her time to selling, much to the chagrin of her parents. For two years straight, she outsold every other salesperson we had in Pennsylvania. Now Judy is a manager in New York. Needless to say, she has improved upon her previous teacher's salary by a very wide margin.

Since I first met Judy, I've hired and worked with many saleswomen who've proven again and again what tremendous opportunities sales can offer to women. Now I have a new philosophy. I say, "*Women*, get out of the kitchen. Get out of the bedroom. Get into sales!" Direct sales is a wonderful chance to develop an exciting, fulfilling career that offers limitless opportunities.

STEVEN HILL: MINORITIES TRY SALES

Today, Steven Hill is my regional manager in Indianapolis, Indiana. He first came to work for me when I was building a staff in the Queens section of New York City. He didn't make a very good first impression. Steven was a skinny Puerto Rican kid. He didn't own a car, and his clothes were completely inappropriate for big-ticket, professional selling. Still, I recognized in Steven something that you couldn't see on the surface—he had guts.

After I hired him, Steven hitchhiked into work every morning. He'd then ride with any other salesman who was willing to give him a lift. I'd often see Steven hitchhiking as I drove in to the office, so I got into the habit of stopping and picking him up. I soon realized that Steven had too much pride to allow me to do that continually. If he'd see me coming, he'd hide behind bushes or signs until I passed by. Steven didn't want a handout; he wanted to work, and earn his keep.

One day, Steven's manager told me that he was thinking about firing him, and asked me for my opinion. "That Hill kid'll never make it," he said. "He doesn't have a car, he doesn't know how to dress…he just doesn't have what it takes." I wasn't ready to give up on him that easily. I told the manager to wait a while until I worked with this young man. I took Steven out into the field and personally trained him in the fundamentals of selling. I helped him get a car and new clothes. Steven became a great salesman. His courage, coupled with the appropriate selling skills, gave him the edge he needed to get ahead. Today, he drives a big Cadillac, dresses like a millionaire, and has a crew of successful salespeople working for him. Steven had decided to change his life. He decided that he should be paid what he knew in his heart he was really worth. He didn't let anything stand in his way. He realized his goals and made a success of himself in the best way possible—through direct sales.

THE PRINCIPLE OF THE ONE-CALL CLOSER

I have always been fascinated by the one-call closer. If you can sell on one call, you free yourself to just sell, travel, and make money. I believe everyone benefits from this process.

Closing a sale during a single call is a goal for some salesmen, and a dream for many others. For me, it's a key element in my sales philosophy. I firmly believe that being a one-call closer and being able to make sales calls without appointments have been vital elements in my success. Let's take a closer look at this issue, and see how it can make any professional salesperson more successful than ever before.

I've been selling for a long time, and have talked with lots of salespeople, so I've got a pretty good idea how most products and services are sold. However, since I'm most familiar with the sign business, let's look at an example from that field.

The typical custom sign sale goes through a process that is something like this:

Step One: The prospective customer looks in the Yellow Pages and calls a few sign companies to come out and give him quotes.

Step Two: Several salespeople pay a visit to the customer's place of business and get a general idea of what the customer needs.

Step Three: The salespeople return to their offices. There, they have an art sketch of the sign drawn up, and estimate a price.

Step Four: The salespeople visit the prospective customer once again to present the designs and the prices.

Step Five: One or more of the salespeople return to their offices once again to revise the art and recalculate prices to accommodate the customer's budget.

Step Six: Finally, one or more of the salespeople return to the customer's place of business with the revised art and price quotes to attempt to close the sale.

Industry statistics show that the average custom sign is sold only after seven to nine calls by a variety of salespeople. Who do you imagine ultimately pays for all those calls, art sketches, and quotes? The customer, of course! To earn a reasonable profit, the seller must prorate the cost of the sales effort into the bottom-line price of any product. Recent research shows that 60 to 70 percent of a custom sign's price is the cost of selling the sign! Everything I've learned about selling tells me that these percentages apply to other businesses as well. Now, think about what would happen if you developed a system that would let you sell your product on *one* call by just *one* salesperson:

1. The customer would win. He or she would be able to buy the product at a *much* lower price, or buy more of the product or a significantly better product for the same price.

2. The salesperson would win. He or she could sell the product for less, and therefore be much more competitive. Salespeople could use their time much more efficiently and productively. They could spend much more time doing what they're supposed to be doing—selling.

3. The company would win. When salespeople are out selling rather than making callbacks, it naturally increases the company's sales volume and lowers overall costs.

If you're already a salesperson or are considering entering the profession, consider with me, if you will, the possibilities and the benefits of one-call selling:

The first is *freedom*. When you work from appointment to appointment, someone else is deciding when and where you'll work. If you can sell without an appointment on a one-call basis, you're totally free.

The second benefit is *opportunity*. I've been selling from coast to coast for many years. I've sold products ranging in price from a few hundred to several thousand dollars. I typically require a twenty-five to fifty percent deposit. With all of these price and deposit requirements, I've *never* found it necessary to make a callback. I've learned that large-ticket items *can* be sold on a one-call, no appointment basis. In fact, I believe that most of my success as a direct salesman is directly attributable to the fact that I've never made a callback! I figure that for every order I've ever lost because I refused to come back for a second visit, I've sold ten orders that I'd have lost if I'd been willing to return.

The rule I've developed and applied over all my years as a direct salesman goes something like this: If customers want my product badly enough, they'll buy it now. If the customer isn't willing to buy my product now, I don't want to sell it to him or her. I'll find another customer. NO EXCEPTIONS!

If *you* want to be a one-call, no-appointment salesperson, keep the following points in mind:

1. Stick to it. If you don't hold to the no-callback rule, you'll never really know if you could have made a sale on your first—and only—call. You'll also never develop the strength of will you need to sell on one call.

2. Callbacks are fundamentally illogical. Customers never get hotter about your product after you leave...they only get colder. As they cool down, they think of all sorts of reasons not to buy.

3. No other professional would ever work twice as long on a project as originally planned and still accept the same fee in payment for services rendered. When mechanics, plumbers, or lawyers work two days instead of one, they earn twice the money, right? Are we, as salespeople, any less professional than mechanics, plumbers, or lawyers?

4. If you've come back once, or if you made a call with an appointment, it becomes difficult or even impossible not to agree to set another appointment...for another time-consuming and expensive callback.

5. People buy only because they recognize the *value* offered by a product or service. They buy when the benefits of that product or service exceed the price. If the perceived value doesn't exceed the price, customers offer objections. Those objections often have nothing to do with their real reasons for rejecting your offer. Therefore, coming back after those specific objections are resolved may not move you any closer to making the sale.

6. Callbacks waste your time. Your customer doesn't care about the fact that you're trying to make a living and have to organize your time as productively as possible. Also, many customers ask you to come back only because they don't have the heart to say no then and there. Occasionally, customers

do think they will buy if you make the second call. During the "cool down" period between calls, however, they find reasons to change their minds...and end up deciding against the purchase.

7. The best reason to make the sale in a single call is that most products can be sold that way. The formula is very simple:

a. The salesperson must build value until it exceeds the price in the customer's mind.

b. The salesperson must give the customer a logical reason to buy now. I've often seen customers produce checkbooks they'd told me they didn't have, almost as if by magic. They'll disregard any disapproval from their spouses or associates, and money seems to materialize out of nowhere. This happens only because I've ignored objections and built value.

Are there any down sides to being a one-call closer? Only one. The salesperson has to have the guts it takes to make the one-call close stick! After all, it's safer to work by making appointments; you have less chance of facing immediate rejection that way. It's also easier to agree to come back for a second call than to insist on a yes or no answer on the spot...and to be tough enough to take the answer you receive.

Try something like this the next time a customer asks you to come back for a second visit: "Mr. Customer, I really don't want to come back again because you might forget about what this can do for you. You might cool down and change your mind. If you don't buy now you might talk yourself out of it, right? Is that really what you want to happen? I'd rather get a yes or no from you now, O.K.?" Many customers who hear this will appreciate your candor as well as your efficiency.

A good salesman can always sell on one call in a professional and friendly manner. I'm convinced that most salespeople would double their incomes if they would develop a one-call, no appointment approach, and stick to it. Give it a try!

STEVE'S FURNITURE

Bobby Lee, my guitar-playing, singing salesman and I called on a furniture store in southern Ohio one day. Now, this wasn't your everyday furniture store. The owner had a huge stuffed gorilla standing in the window scowling at everyone who passed by. I decided, for some reason, that I had to own that gorilla.

Our sale seemed impossible right from the start. The customer, who was named Steve, told us that he'd seen two salesmen from our company just the day before. In fact, he told us, he still remembered their presentation. I thought for a moment, and then told Steve that I was a famous salesman, and that he should give me a chance to put on the same presentation...so that he could see how it *should* have been done. I told him, "Steve, you can learn a lot about selling just by watching me, even if you don't buy." Steve was a competitive fellow and quickly accepted the challenge. He smiled and agreed to take another look. He seemed intrigued by the idea of comparing two presentations for the same product, and watching someone with such a big ego.

As Bobby Lee and I talked with him, I was amazed to discover that Steve really did know a lot about our presentation. The only part he had missed was the part where we *build a lot of value.* I started by making him see his name up in lights. Then, I made him visualize other people seeing that same name up in lights. Soon I had him seeing customers coming into his store who might otherwise have passed him by. I made him want the sign.

When my presentation was over, I'd sold him a sign for more than the price he'd been quoted by the other salesman the day before...*and* I also got the stuffed gorilla! But the story didn't end there. As we started writing up the order, Steve said, "Tell you what. I want two signs. I want one for this store, and I want another one for my wife's store next door. Let's go next door now, and my wife will give you a check."

When we visited Steve's wife in the second store, she looked at him with a stunned gaze. "I thought we voted yesterday not to buy new signs until spring!" she said. "Yeah, I know," Steve said, "but those guys yesterday...they lost control. Now, *these* guys have control. Write 'em a check."

With that statement, Steve put into words what most salespeople and customers never realize. People buy goods and services when a salesperson gains and maintains control, builds value, and creates enough urgency to make the sale happen. When salespeople lose control, they don't sell, no matter how hard they try.

Think of it this way: Customers have the *right* to be sold to when you call on them! As we've noted before, if you take your car to a mechanic, you expect him to be able to fix it. When you go to a doctor, you expect that the doctor will know how to make you feel better. In the same way, if a customer agrees to talk to you and let you make a presentation, he or she should reasonably expect that you have the skill to make the sale.

If you're one of those salespeople who feel compelled to make several calls before you close any sale, maybe your customers need a new salesperson...one who can save them time and trouble by getting the job done on *one* call.

TALES OF THE ONE-CALL CLOSER

One day, early in my sales career, I called on a large cooperative produce market in South Bend, Indiana. The place was buzzing as I walked in, and the president of the corporation said that he was just too busy to talk with me. It was obvious that they needed a sign, so I convinced him to give me just a few minutes for a short preview of my presentation. Well, the president and several of his associates became so engrossed in my presentation that their time limitations started slipping away. We all became deeply involved in building value, visualizing benefits, and seeing a big, new sign materialize in front of the building.

The presentation moved ahead smoothly. Soon we were at the point where I asked for an order and a deposit. All of a sudden, we had a problem. This business, it turned out, was managed by a twelve-member board of directors. This board, which made all major purchasing decisions, met only on Wednesday evenings. Today was Friday. "Sorry," the president said, "but rules are rules. We'll just have to wait 'til Wednesday for a decision on this." After a short pause I said that I understood and that I wished we could have done business. As I packed up, it became evident to them that I had no intention of returning again the following week.

When I finished packing, I said wistfully, "You know, sometimes we give discounts to small businesses for doing business with us on one call. Now, I'm sure a big company like you wouldn't be interested, but let's figure it out, anyway." Here the showman in me cranked into high gear. With some flourishes of the pen, I hummed a quiet tune and figured out this "one-call discount." When I finished, I looked at the figures and said, "Wow, that's a lot of money!"

I showed the president my work sheet and pointed with my pen. "Now this," I said, "is next Wednesday's price." Needless to say, it was high. I looked at my prospective customer in the eye. "However, if you hand me a check for two thousand dollars ...outside of that door in the next fifteen minutes, this'll be *today's* price." It was much lower. "Anyway, thanks for your time." I stepped out the door and had a cup of coffee.

After a few minutes had passed, the door of the office opened, and the president walked over to me. He handed me a check for two thousand dollars, made out in my name. He winked and said, "We know what you did in there. You weren't fooling anyone. But what the hey...we wanted that sign, so you just made our job easier for us."

I've made similar sales to corporations with boards that were supposed to vote on all purchasing decisions, churches that needed a consensus of deacons and the opinion of the congregation, and lodges that had to poll the membership...ALL ON ONE CALL. It *can* be done. Think it through, work up the courage, and you'll usually find a way to be a one-call closer.

THOMPSON'S MUSIC COMPANY

One fine spring day, Steven Hill and I were driving through the beautiful state of Kentucky. This was the part of the country where I'd sold a lot when I started my career as a direct salesman, so while we sought out new prospects, I'd also stop in and visit some of my old customers. Those visits are always a pleasure. It is almost like a family reunion. I was also getting a kick out of introducing Steve to this beautiful territory, since he'd never been in this state before. We were both having a great time.

One of my salesmen back in Chicago had a daughter who'd just started taking violin lessons. I'd promised him that I'd keep my eyes open for a quality violin that he could give her. With my promise in mind, I began looking for a music store that needed a sign. As we passed through a small town, I found just the place I was looking for—Thompson's Music Company.

This place filled the bill perfectly, I thought. It certainly needed a sign, and they had what I was looking for. An arrangement of fine-looking violins was displayed right there in the front window. Steven and I pulled in, picked up our sample kits, and walked in.

Mr. Thompson was a friendly guy, but he gave us some bad news as we introduced ourselves. Once again, one of our salespeople had already been in to see him...not once, but *six times*! Mr. Thompson said he figured he'd buy from that salesman one of these days, but he wasn't ready to make a commitment now.

Here, I thought, is a perfect example of why I teach my people never to make callbacks. The salesman who'd called on Thompson six times without a sale had *proven* that they just don't work! Now, I was determined to prove he could be sold to on one call if it were done right. Steven and I told Mr. Thompson that we wanted to show him the sign he should buy...when he was ready, of course. I casually mentioned that I might be in the market for a violin, as well.

Selling to Mr. Thompson was easy. He needed a sign, and he knew it. He *wanted* a sign, but hadn't been given the proper reasons and motivation to make the purchase. By the time Steven and I had finished building value for this customer, he knew just how much he really wanted and needed what we had to offer. All we had to do was give him a logical reason to buy *now*. I did this by telling Mr. Thompson that if he'd buy the sign, I'd buy a violin. That was enough reason for him; the deal was done.

After *both* sales, Steven commented to Mr. Thompson that he'd made a really great deal. Apparently Mr. Thompson thought so, too. Maybe Steven overdid it a bit praising Mr. Thompson's bargaining skills. As we were walking out the door, the owner called us back into his store. "I'm sorry, I just can't do this. I can't let you guys have *that* violin after what you've done for me," he said. He reached behind him and produced a beautiful, handcrafted instrument. "Here," he said, "I want you to have the best violin I've got in the shop." He took back the first violin and gave us this much more expensive one at no extra cost.

Always remember:

1. Value sells a product or service.

2. When the value exceeds the price, customers buy.

3. If a customer wants your product or service badly enough he or she will find a way to come up with the money.

4. If you're their *customer* as well as a salesperson, you'll be treated with more respect.

5. There is *never* a good reason for a one-call salesperson to make two or more calls.

CREATIVE SELLING

Creative salespeople make magic happen. They're able to use words and gestures as powerful selling tools. In a limited amount of time, creative salespeople can strengthen or rekindle the dreams of their customers, and incorporate their products or services into those dreams. Creative salespeople can make their customers visualize themselves using the product, and also visualize their peers, family, competitors, and friends seeing them enjoy the benefits the product offers.

> *The essence of creative selling is to find out what is of value to your customer, and then incorporate that value into your product or service.*

When the creative salesperson has the customer seeing, feeling, and thinking about the product or service in the proper way, he can then use his or her imagination to give that customer a logical reason to *buy now*.

THE ACCESSORY STORE

One example of how creative selling techniques have helped me make hundreds of sales occurred a while back when Jimmy Thumper and I were selling in New Jersey. We hadn't sold together for a while, so we were reminiscing, selling signs, making money, and generally enjoying ourselves. One afternoon we called on a business that sold a variety of household items such as spas, fireplaces, and lawn furniture. George, the owner of this store, was about the toughest customer I've ever run into. He was abrasive, opinionated, and he didn't want to listen to a sales pitch; he wanted us to get right to the bottom line.

George kept interrupting me as I tried to make my presentation. Finally, we were ready to make our proposition. I nudged Jimmy and whispered, "Hey, let's have some fun here, O.K.?" Jimmy winked, and we were on our way. I plugged in my sign sample and jumped up onto a nearby table with the lighted sign over my head. I shouted, "Gather 'round, folks...the show is about to begin!" Customers and store staff looked over at me, wondering what all the commotion was about. Soon they started gathering around us. As they shoved and laughed, I started my speech.

First, I built value aggressively. I talked about new customers coming to the store, greater profits, paying the rent, and so on. Then I made them visualize George's competitors looking at him with envy. Then, I asked the audience if they thought George needed a new sign. I wasn't surprised when everyone agreed that he did. It was at that moment that I noticed a mailman standing at the edge of the crowd. I asked him if he'd ever missed George's place. He said, "Oh, yeah…it took me a while to find it at first." Thanks, my friend, I thought to myself. I said, "George, even the mailman can't find you." Everyone laughed. Finally, I asked everyone gathered around to vote on whether or not George should buy a new sign. They gave me a unanimous yes.

As all this was going on, George stood by silently. It dawned on him that he wasn't in control of the situation. I said to him, "George, all these people seem to think you need a sign. I think you need a sign, and I'm not getting down from here until you agree to buy the darn sign. So tell me, George…how close am I to selling you one?" George folded his arms and said, "Well, you're getting closer, but I'm not buying one." "Why not?" I demanded. "Money," George said. "You're asking for too much money."

That, of course, was the answer I was hoping for. I replied, "Well, George, if money's your only problem, let me help you out. Why the hell did you let me get up here and make a fool out of myself for money?" At that point, I pulled out a big roll of hundred-dollar bills. There was ten thousand dollars in that roll. I counted off eight bills. I slowly dropped them on the table, and Jimmy picked them up. He then deducted that amount from the price we'd quoted. I said, "I'll need six hundred down. You think you can manage that much, George?"

George smiled for the first time. His exact words were, "Give that man a check for six hundred dollars. That show was worth six hundred even if I never see that damn sign! I've been in business for fourteen years. I've read books about professional salesmen and heard about them all my life. You're the first really professional salesman I've ever met."

Now, don't get me wrong…I'm not advocating jumping up on tables every day to demonstrate your product. I've actually only done that a few times over the years. However, what I *am* advocating is this:

1. Practice and perfect your presentation. Be sure that you know it so well that you'd feel comfortable if you ever did stand on a table and present it to a crowd of strangers.

2. Study salesmanship to the point where you'll be able to recognize when it would be appropriate to use this or any other selling tactic, and make it work. As I've said before, all the world's a stage, and salespeople are the actors. Why not be a highly paid actor?

*Sam Golden, onetime president of Gulf Development, Inc., awarding
me a trophy for breaking a sales volume record in New York City*

Standing in front of my sales empire. I hired, trained, and promoted sales managers and then moved on to start somewhere else.

Number one in the Grand Ol' Opry Hotel in 1989

Recognition is mostly what salespeople strive for. Good salespeople both give and get it.

Good salespeople can live the good life. Fishing in Baja California, near La Paz, Mexico. We made sushi out of the yellowtail.

Kings is as kings does. I receive a royal welcome after breaking some more sales records.

My two great loves – my lovely wife, Machiko, and my good dog, Rex

Rex is always ready to stand in for Batman, Superman, Tyson, or J. Paul Getty. Here he tries to decide whether to make some deals or put the bite on the Joker.

*It doesn't have to be lonely out there on the road. Every now and then
you meet the most interesting people.*

My first sale with Gulf. From then on I never had a bad day in sales.

Lloyd Allard
New World Record Breaker

When we had Regional Manager Lloyd Allard's picture on the cover of the Road Runner in February as the 1981 Regional Manager of the Year, little did we know that before many months were over, he would again be featured but this time as the new World Record holder not of one but of four National Sales Records.

For the month of August, Lloyd broke Dave Baltes' record of Personal Sales (set only last April) for a new grand total of $111,698 for the month. In addition, he broke the record set by RM Ray Clark way back in 1969 with 58 Contracts sold by an individual. His own Symbol Sign record of 44 sales was increased to 66. And finally, Dave Baltes' Big Sig 37 total was surpassed with a new record of 48.

Let's just total what Lloyd did in the month:

58 Contracts
48 Big Sigs
66 Symbol Signs
$111,698 Volume

During the month he had:

A $8669 Week Earnings
A $5125 Week Earnings
A $4216 Week Earnings
A $3750 Week Earnings
A $1486 Week Earnings

With:

6 $1000 Days Earnings
1 $2000 Day Earnings

Published Monthly by:
GULF DEVELOPMENT, INC.
Bill Zimmerman, Editor

22309 S. Western Avenue
Torrance, California
Zip Code 90501
Phone (213) 320-8210

Good sales principles work all the time, anywhere

Part of my scrapbook

NEWS & VIEWS

Lloyd Allard #1 Division Manager
1985, 1986, 1987 & 1988

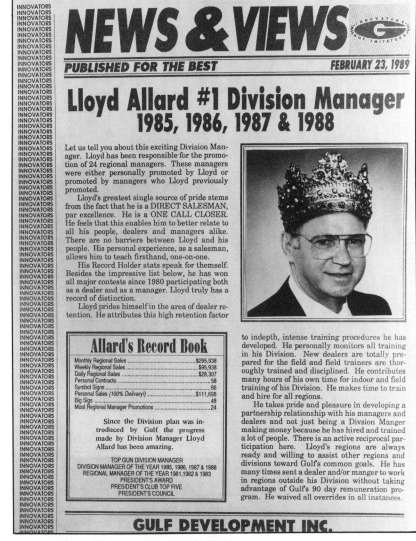

Let us tell you about this exciting Division Manager. Lloyd has been responsible for the promotion of 24 regional managers. These managers were either personally promoted by Lloyd or promoted by managers who Lloyd previously promoted.

Lloyd's greatest single source of pride stems from the fact that he is a DIRECT SALESMAN, par excellence. He is a ONE CALL CLOSER. He feels that this enables him to better relate to all his people, dealers and managers alike. There are no barriers between Lloyd and his people. His personal experience, as a salesman, allows him to teach firsthand, one-on-one.

His Record Holder stats speak for themself. Besides the impressive list below, he has won all major contests since 1980 participating both as a dealer and as a manager. Lloyd truly has a record of distinction.

Lloyd prides himself in the area of dealer retention. He attributes this high retention factor to indepth, intense training procedures he has developed. He personally monitors all training in his Division. New dealers are totally prepared for the field and field trainers are thoroughly trained and disciplined. He contributes many hours of his own time for indoor and field training of his Division. He makes time to train and hire for all regions.

He takes pride and pleasure in developing a partnership relationship with his managers and dealers and not just being a Divsion Manger making money because he has hired and trained a lot of people. There is an active reciprocal participation here. Lloyd's regions are always ready and willing to assist other regions and divisions toward Gulf's common goals. He has many times sent a dealer and/or manger to work in regions outside his Division without taking advantage of Gulf's 90 day remuneration program. He waived all overrides in all instances.

Allard's Record Book

Monthly Regional Sales	$295,938
Weekly Regional Sales	$95,938
Daily Regional Sales	$28,307
Personal Contracts	58
Symbol Signs	66
Personal Sales *(100% Delivery!)*	$111,698
Big Sigs	48
Most Regional Manager Promotions	24

Since the Division plan was introduced by Gulf the progress made by Division Manager Lloyd Allard has been amazing.

TOP GUN DIVISION MANAGER
DIVISION MANAGER OF THE YEAR 1985, 1986, 1987 & 1988
REGIONAL MANAGER OF THE YEAR 1981,1982 & 1983
PRESIDENT'S AWARD
PRESIDENT'S CLUB TOP FIVE
PRESIDENT'S COUNCIL

GULF DEVELOPMENT INC.

Good selling principles are consistent. If you work hard and apply the correct selling techniques, you will always be a winner.

News & Views

Published For The Gulf Family March 29, 1990

Allard #1 Division Manager for 1989

LLOYD ALLARD
DIVISION VICE PRESIDENT

Division Manager of the Year
1985, 1986, 1987, 1988, 1989

We are proud to salute Division Vice President Lloyd Allard for his leadership in 1989. Lloyd is one of the most dynamic and versatile employees here at Gulf Development. Gulf has taken Lloyd on a whirlwind tour of the United States during his duty with Gulf. He has just started up his second Division in New Orleans, Louisiana, a far cry from his original territory on the west coast.

Lloyd originally joined Gulf in California rocketing to the number one spot of Regional Manager. Gulf then asked Lloyd to move to New York where he established another solid Region base. His next assignments with Gulf took him to Boston, Columbus, and Memphis. He was finally grounded in Chicago where he duplicated his earlier successes with Gulf and formed a Division base and Regional Training Center for many of his Division Regional Managers. With the training center running smoothly and the experience under his belt, Lloyd was asked to head up a new Division in New Orleans, Louisiana.

Lloyd starts recruitment in his new home base on April 1st. What a guy! No wonder his loyal subjects refer to him as the "King." Lloyd's records stand for themselves. He still holds the record for the most Regional Manager promotions. . . 26 and counting! These managers were either personally promoted by Lloyd or promoted by managers who Lloyd previously promoted.

Lloyd prides himself in the area of dealer retention. He attributes this high retention factor to indepth, intense training procedures he has developed. He personally monitors all training in his Divisions. New dealers are totally prepared for the field and field trainers are thoroughly trained and disciplined. He contributes many hours of his own time for indoor and field training of his Division. He makes time to train and hire for all regions.

1989 was a great year for Lloyd and subsequently for Gulf. Congratulations Lloyd, now we're looking to you to herald in the beginning of a great decade for Gulf Development.

❖❖❖❖

GULF DEVELOPMENT INC.

Success speaks for itself

CHAPTER 4

Principles of Selling

True principles remain constant. Selling, just like playing golf, fishing, flying an airplane, and building a fire, is governed by many principles. The more closely you adhere to those principles, the more successful you will be. If you violate the principles of selling, it will be difficult for you to ever succeed.

Many of the principles you'll encounter on the following pages will seem obvious to you—and they should! Consider them carefully, though. Quite often, the most obvious truths are the ones we overlook or forget. Like most truths, the most simple are often the most profound.

INTRODUCTION

Put the correct ingredients into a bowl, mix them together, and then bake them at the right temperature for the right amount of time and you'll end up with a delicious cake. The more you practice making them, the better your cakes will be. Selling works the same way. To become a successful salesperson, there's much to learn and a lot of hard work to do. However, if you study the principles that make a sale work—the ingredients of your cake—and if you apply these principles properly and frequently enough, you'll succeed in sales.

The more you practice, the harder you work, the better you'll become at your profession. I hope the principles you'll find in this section will help *you* become a better salesperson.

BUILDING VALUE

The most important ingredient in any "sale mix" is *value.*
Value, often called "benefits," is the only reason that anybody
ever buys anything. When you build the value of your product in
your customer's mind, you create the magic that makes any sale
possible. Remember:

Finding out what is of value to your customer, and incor-
porating that value into your product, is the essence of
salesmanship.

Building the value of your product or service in the mind
of your customer is the heart of any sales presentation.

Let's look at this process closely and analyze it at the different
levels of selling. As we do, I want you to consider these questions:

What *is* value?

How do you effectively build value into any product or
service?

How can you cause your customer to recognize the value
of the product or service you're offering?

Let's start at the beginning....

LEVEL 1: CONSTRUCTION

Whenever you deal with the sale of any tangible, manufactured product, you probably hear more about the construction
of that product than anything else.

Salespeople go on for far too long about things like thickness,
brightness, durability, paint, guarantees, and all the other issues
related to the construction of a product. Of course, every good
salesperson *does* have to know all of this information. In fact, he
or she has to know *everything there is to know* about the product.
The salesperson, as I've stated before, has to become an expert
about every feature of the products he or she sells. The *great*
salesperson, however, understands that construction and features do *not* sell the product. As the wise old salesman says,

"Construction does not lead to seduction!" Only amateurs try to sell by focusing their attention on the weakest selling points of their products.

LEVEL 2: FEATURES

Features are, after construction, the second most often talked about characteristic of a product. Here again, I don't believe that many products are ever sold on the basis of features. Great salespeople always master all aspects of construction and fully understand the features of their products. They thoroughly familiarize themselves with these elements to use them as a platform from which they can move on to discuss value or benefits—the *real* reasons why people buy.

LEVEL 3: VALUE, OR BENEFITS

No matter what you buy, you do so only because of the benefits you get from it. There are countless varieties of ways in which any product or service can benefit a customer. Consider this general rule about how to build value when you sell:

Most salespeople try to convince their customers that they should buy a product or service because of the benefits the *salesperson* thinks are important. Great salespeople, on the other hand, discover which benefits are important to the customer, and then convince the customer that he or she will derive those benefits from the product or service they are offering.

LEVEL 4: VISUALIZING VALUE

Great salespeople can take this process one step further. They not only convince their customers that they'll derive the benefits they want from the product or service, but they also make it possible for the customer to *visualize* himself enjoying that value.

In the sign business, for example, we usually start out by telling our customers that a new sign will increase business. This is a good approach, and might be enough to sell the product on its own. However, when we can cause these customers to *see* new patrons coming in and bringing new business with them, they probably *will* buy. When customers can see, feel, and experience the value and the benefits they'll obtain from your product or service, they're much easier to sell to. Whether you're selling books, boats, signs, cars, or any other product, this principle always works in exactly the same way.

LEVEL 5: THE ADVANCED SALESPERSON

The advanced salesperson enhances this process by taking it still one step further. He or she is able to make customers visualize *others* seeing him or her enjoy the value or benefits that the product offers. When salespeople can use all of their acting skills to make this extended visualization happen, the sky's the limit. Salespeople who can make a customer see his peers, his enemies, or his family looking at him as he enjoys the benefits of the product have tapped into the most powerful motivating force of all—the human ego.

People will spend money more readily to satisfy their egos than for any other reason. They'll make almost any sacrifice necessary to obtain this kind of satisfaction. Where people's egos are concerned, they tend to overlook the normal caution and reluctance associated with making buying decisions.

Finally, when it comes to matters of the ego, purchases don't have to make strict "dollars and sense." Consider monogrammed shirts, for example. People don't buy them because they look better, last longer, or fit more nicely than other shirts. They buy them because they are *personalized* and make an ego statement that satisfies the owner.

Making customers visualize other people seeing them enjoy the benefits of a product is professional selling at its best. It's good salesmanship to convince a mother that her son will do better in school if he uses your books. If you can make that mother see her friends marvelling at how well her son is doing, and attributing that success to her purchase of your books, it's fantastic. Convincing a customer that he'll enjoy the boat you're selling is great, but if you can make him see all his friends jealously watching him enjoy it, you've probably sold the boat. This technique works. I've used it myself to close sales in hundreds of seemingly impossible situations.

OVERCOMING OBJECTIONS

As anyone in the business will tell you, overcoming objections is a big part of any salesperson's job. A great deal has been said and much has been written on the subject. Let me now share a few of my thoughts on this topic.

First, great salespeople get very few objections during their presentations. A common misconception is that good salespeople are able to handle objections more successfully than others. While this is fundamentally true, it focuses on the wrong side of the issue. Generally speaking, an objection arises only when the salesperson mishandles his or her presentation. Arnold Palmer isn't a great golfer because he can successfully get out of a sand trap. He's a great golfer because he knows how to avoid getting into sand traps in the first place. When you, the salesperson, approach your customers appropriately, you'll hear very few objections.

Every objection a customer poses cannot only be answered, but can also be transformed into a sound reason why the customer should buy. This technique just takes a little thought, planning, and practice. I've used it myself for years. I often ask my salespeople to share with me some of the objections they've heard. I then teach them how they could have turned that "objection" into a solid reason why the customer should buy. I've never been stumped. By thinking and planning ahead, the great salesperson can turn any objection around.

Still, turning around an objection will never make a sale in and of itself. People raise objections when they don't want to buy, or when they feel the need to protect themselves. In fact, customers frequently don't even tell you what their real reason for not buying is. If you handle one objection, providing a resolution to the problem the customer has raised, customers often manage to find new objections until the "no sale" message is communicated. However, if a customer wants a product badly enough, he or she will concentrate on all the reasons to buy rather than on the reasons not to buy. The truth is that anyone can be sold to, and overcoming objections is really a very small part of the total selling process.

There are, in fact, only a few fundamental objections, and there are hundreds of variations of them. If you know how to manage these basic types of objections, you're certain to do well in sales. Some of the most common objections you'll hear include "I don't have the money," "I'm too busy to look now," "I've got to ask my wife," "I've got to check with my accountant," and so on. Always remember that there's nothing you can do to solve any of these problems. What you *can* do, however, is to make the customer want your product so badly that he'll find a way to come up with the money to make the purchase. When you make him see the value of the product with crystal clarity, he'll buy what you have to offer even if it means catching it from the wife or the accountant!

RAY'S AUTO REPAIR

Franchesca is a hard-working saleswoman who works out of our Chicago office. Recently she was promoted to the position of district manager. On that occasion, I asked her what I could do to help her celebrate her advancing sales career. Without missing a beat, she said that rather than me giving her a gift or taking her out to dinner, what she *really* wanted was to accompany me on a sales call. That was fine with me, so off we went looking for a prospect.

We stopped at a small shop in Milwaukee called Ray's Auto Repair. Ray was a classic case of the hard-to-sell customer. He hit us with a laundry list of reasons why he couldn't buy a sign. These included:

1. "I can't afford it."

2. "I'm not sure the landlord would let me put a sign up."

3. "I'd have to break up 30 feet of concrete to put in electrical lines."

4. "I'm not sure how long I'll be at this location."

5. "Everyone already knows me."

6. "I really don't like signs."

7. "My wife would object to it."

And that wasn't the end of it. Ray came up with many more detailed and creative objections that I can't recall anymore. I finally suggested to Ray that he take a look at something new I had to offer just in case he ever did need a sign. He agreed to look, and I launched into my presentation. As I built the value of a new sign, things gradually began to change. Suddenly, Ray offered us coffee and began treating us like old friends. Suddenly, Ray told us that he *had* been giving some thought to getting a new sign after all. We talked to him about the obvious benefits the sign would bring—new customers, more money, and all the rest. We also talked about how all of Ray's friends, family, and peers would see his name up there on a big, lighted sign. We soon had Ray seeing all of his friends...and his enemies...marvelling at his new image.

Suddenly, finding the money was no problem, and Ray's wife had nothing to do with the decision. Suddenly, the installation and the electrical hook-up were child's play. The sale became routine, and we closed with little difficulty and with no objections. As we left Ray's shop, Franchesca turned to me and said, "Darn, Mr. Allard, that was too easy. I was hoping to see you sell a *tough* one. I wanted to see you get on a roll!"

The fact is that if you sell properly, almost all sales look easy. My son is a Green Beret stationed at Fort Campbell, Kentucky. Some time ago, he was riding with me and watching me sell. Naturally, I was showing off for him, selling lots of signs and earning a lot of money. Later, we were at an office staff meeting and my son was introduced. Someone asked him how he felt about watching his famous father sell. My son is not a salesman, so they all looked easy to him. He commented that he hadn't noticed anything unusual. The sales were easy and routine as far as he was concerned. "I don't know," he said. "Dad's just the luckiest bastard I ever saw. Everyone he talks to seems to want to buy a sign." That's always the way it is with good salespeople...they always *look* lucky!

The objections your customers offer are a reflection of his or her worries and fears. Like 99 percent of our own worries and fears, these concerns are usually insubstantial and never materialize into real problems. When people want to do something badly enough, they find ways to overcome their own worries and fears. If you make your customer want your product or service badly enough, he'll overcome his own objections.

DISCOUNTING THE PRICE

From time to time, almost every salesperson makes a sale by offering a price discount. In most direct sales programs, this tactic is a significant part of the selling process. In my opinion, it is also one of the most misunderstood and abused selling tools available to us. Most salespeople think that lowering the price will, in and of itself, sell the product. They lower their price too soon, too often, and by too much. In many cases, the very fact that the salesperson has lowered the price ends up *preventing* the sale rather than clinching it. Because price discounting is such an important part of our business, we must thoroughly understand the principles that govern the effective application of this potentially powerful sales tool.

Here are four principles that would make most salespeople much more successful:

1. Raise the value of your product like a spendthrift.

2. Lower the price of your product like a miser.

3. Build value liberally and often.

4. Lower your price reluctantly and sparingly.

When customers don't want a product, they'll usually tell you that the price is too high even if price has nothing to do with their decision. Lowering your price doesn't make them change their mind because price isn't the issue. On the other hand, when a customer *wants* a product, he or she will come up with the money one way or another.

I've often sold signs to customers that had already been visited by one of our salespeople, and I'd sell these signs for a higher price than the previous salesperson had quoted for exactly the same product. These other salespeople had tried to get the customer to buy something he didn't want by lowering the price. My approach was to first make the customer want the product by building value to the point where he was willing to pay almost any price for it.

Often it's a lot easier to build value than to lower your price. Why? It's simple: Whenever you lower the price of a product, you also automatically lower the value of the product in your customer's mind.

Consider this example: If you were buying a diamond, what factors would affect the value you placed on the stone? First, you'd consider your own general impression of the diamond. Second, you would evaluate the confidence you have in the salesperson showing you the diamond, and what he or she tells you. Third, you would consider the price being asked for the diamond.

If the price of the diamond were lower, the value you place on it would also be less. This applies to any product that's ever offered for sale, whether it's diamonds, cars, houses, or signs. Lowering prices without building value is often a downward spiral that ultimately leads to frustration and lost opportunity. Building value, on the other hand, often creates added credibility for you, your product, and your company by making your product more desirable.

The formula here is simple: Always build more value before you lower the price! Lowering the price may create urgency, but it also lowers value. Do it carefully.

Here's another important point to keep in mind about lowering your price—a point that's often overlooked by salespeople. Your customer will never believe that you're giving him a bargain unless he's able to see how the transaction benefits *you* also. The customer must be convinced that you will benefit from the transaction just as he or she will. Remember, your customers are intelligent. They will never believe that you're Santa Claus. Show them how you will still benefit, and they'll believe you're giving them a special bargain.

One fact about the selling business that's always amused me is that the salesperson, unlike other professionals, charges less money the longer he or she works. After you make a particularly long presentation, why not try *raising* the price of your product instead of lowering it? Try telling your customers that, like all professionals, the longer you work, the more you have to charge. Tell your customers that the meter is running. Remind them that you are a professional rendering a service, and you expect to be paid for your time just like any other professional. And don't be afraid! Remember, the worst thing that can happen is that your customer might say no.

CLOSING THE SALE

Closing is another commonly misunderstood concept of selling. Even many good salespeople who manage other aspects of the sales process very well still misunderstand the mechanics of closing. Many people think of the successful closer as the person who puts a lot of pressure on the customer to get the sale. Actually, a salesperson who puts pressure on a customer is doing so only because he or she doesn't know how to close properly.

Closing isn't difficult when the rest of the sale is handled correctly. When the customer wants the product, likes the price, and understands the terms and conditions of the sale, closing is the logical last step in the process. When you give your customers sound reasons why they should buy now, they usually will.

Never try to pressure your customer into making a commitment to buy. Build value until your customer *knows* he's getting a bargain. Make your proposition clear and straightforward so that he can make a logical decision. Make buying your product a logical and sensible thing to do. At the same time, make *not* buying your product seem like an illogical, foolish thing to do.

The correct formula for closing any sale is as follows:

1. Qualify the customer. Make sure he or she can make the decision to buy without having to consult anyone else.

2. Build value. Make sure your customer wants your product or service so badly that if he doesn't get it, he'll feel as though he's lost something.

3. Clarify. Make sure that your customer understands everything he or she needs to know in order to make an intelligent, informed decision.

4. Create urgency. Give your customer a solid and logical reason to buy your product or service *now*.

5. Practice. As a professional salesperson, you should review and practice the art of closing a sale until you've mastered it perfectly.

URGENCY

A sense of urgency is an essential element in almost every direct sales presentation. This sense usually has two central objectives. They are:

1. To provide the customer with a *reason* to do business now.

2. To provide the customer with an *inducement* to do business now.

Consider these examples:

First, providing a reason to do business now:

"Mr. Customer, I can't come back again next Thursday. I'm going on a two-week business trip and I'll be in Pittsburgh next week. I would have to fly over here just to make the sale."

Second, providing the customer with an inducement to do business now:

"Mr. Customer, if you'll let me write this order up today, I'll make you a very special offer. I'll deduct the price of a round-trip airline ticket to Pittsburgh from the selling price of your product."

If you give it a little thought, you'll find you can build urgency into any closing situation. Of course, the urgency you create must be logical in order for it to be effective.

DRESS LIKE A WINNER

Have you ever heard the old expression "Never judge a book by its cover?" I've often thought about this phrase, and wondered just how anyone can judge a book if not by its cover. For example, if you see a book with a picture of Batman socking the Joker on its cover, you can assume that it's a comic book. We know that a black book with a gold cross on its cover is usually a Bible. We're able to assess something about these books and what they probably contain based on what we see on their exterior covering.

Salespeople, like books, are frequently judged by their "covers." We usually have a very short time to make a good first impression. As I've stated earlier, people naturally tend to treat important-looking people with more respect. They are much more willing to stop what they're doing and listen to a person who really looks rich than one who dresses poorly.

I believe that every salesperson should dress like a millionaire if he or she can. Salespeople should think of the money they spend on clothing as an investment in their career. My experiences have taught me that everyone wants to do business with rich, important people, so I always try to dress in a manner that conveys the message that I'm rich and important. I've found that the whole world is set up this way. If you want to succeed in sales, show the customer that you are someone they should listen to by the way you walk, talk, and dress.

Many people who come into sales start out with a poor wardrobe and very poor dressing habits. They tell themselves that when they make a lot of money, they'll go out and buy some new clothes. Unfortunately, they make the mistake of failing to recognize that their poor wardrobe causes them to stand out as novices, and they significantly diminish their chances of *ever* making any money.

Look at yourself in a full-length mirror and judge yourself critically. Compare yourself to the best-dressed salesperson you know. How do you stack up?

If you can't afford new shoes, polish your old ones. If you can't afford a new suit, clean and press the best clothes you have. Don't wear white socks, and make sure your tie, suit, and belt go together. Men, get a fresh haircut and trim those sideburns. Ladies, style your hair and keep your makeup fresh and professional looking. Also, button that top button on your blouse. Salespeople, always remember—the sales profession is unkind to those who do not prepare.

EVOKING TRUST

I've called on independent businesses for years now. I show the owner my product, and close the sale within an hour. I walk into these businesses as a total stranger, make a sale for an item costing several hundred to several thousand dollars, and I'm never asked to show identification. And there's more. Not only do I make the sale, but I also collect a deposit of several hundred to several thousand dollars, and always ask that the check be made out to me personally. For about one third of these sales, that deposit is made in cash. I have also taught hundreds of salespeople to do the same. How do you evoke this kind of trust from your customers? How does a customer know who I am, or that he can trust me with his money? I never do anything to prove that I am who I say I am. How do I do it? I have a theory that I think will cause your customer to totally trust you.

First, I believe that you evoke trust when you yourself are trustworthy. The Bible says that if you want to make friends, be friendly. Shouldn't that apply to trust in exactly the same way? If you want to be completely trusted, be completely honest. Then, and only then, can you reasonably expect to be trusted.

Second, always remember that as a salesperson, you are a professional whose primary objective should always be to help the customer. Focus on helping your customer more than on making a commission.

Third, expect to be trusted. Never do or say anything to prove you're honest. Assume that what you say can and will be believed without any verification.

Fourth, always talk straight to your customers. Never try to manipulate them. Don't try to use rusty psychological tricks to get your customers to say, do, or think the way you want them to.

Finally, listen carefully to what your customers have to say. You'll impress them with your integrity if you listen. In addition, when you listen carefully, your customers will often tell you exactly how to sell them what you have to offer.

THE WORLD'S MOST POPULAR OBJECTION: "I DON'T HAVE THE MONEY"

The old line "I can't afford it...I don't have the money" has to be the most commonly heard excuse for not buying that every salesperson encounters, regardless of the product or service being offered. All too often, this line kills all prospects for a sale.

If I could guarantee you that every customer you ever see from now on will be able to afford the product or service you're selling, would it be worth the price you paid for this book? Well, I can't quite make that an absolute guarantee, but I *can* give you some tips that'll explain why few, if any, customers are ever *really* too short on cash to buy your product or service.

I have sold to big corporations with million-dollar budgets and mom and pop operations that needed to sell something before they could buy lunch. In all my years in sales, however, I've never met a person who couldn't afford something that he or she really wanted. Oh, sure, I've heard the line "I don't have the money" as many times as any other salesperson. And yes, I've met customers who were struggling to pay their bills. I never really considered that they couldn't buy my product if I made them want it badly enough.

I approach these challenges by playing this little game. I'd create for the customer the mental image of the customer's friend pulling up to his business in a shiny new Rolls Royce. I'd then embroider the scene by having the friend say to the customer, "You can have my Rolls Royce for three hundred dollars." Then I'd try to imagine where the customer would get the money to make this purchase. I couldn't imagine the customer turning his friend down...and neither could the customer!

On other occasions, I'd create a different scene. I'd have the customer imagine his landlord coming into his place of business and saying, "You can stay here rent free for twenty years if you give me a payment today of three hundred dollars." Then, I'd speculate about where this customer would get the three hundred. You and I both know that he'd get it *somewhere*, right?

Now that we both know that the customer can come up with a three-hundred-dollar deposit, I just have to make him want my product as badly as he'd want the Rolls Royce or a rent-free location. If you build value to the point where the customer is convinced that your product or service is as valuable as an expensive car or free real estate, you'll make your sale...and your customer will come up with the money.

When you build enough value, you can sell to anyone. If you ever fail to sell to your customer, be assured that the reason for that failure is that you've failed to build enough value. You will probably never fail to make a sale because your customer can't afford the product or service.

STRAIGHT TALK

Salespeople communicate in many different ways. Their dress, their attitude, and their body language all convey information to prospective customers and clients. Without question, however, the most important means of communication for salespeople is speech. Talk is a salesperson's stock-in-trade. Every salesperson should become a master at the art of verbal communication.

The longer I'm in the direct sales profession, the more I realize how poorly we communicate with one another. I'm absolutely convinced that we understand only half of what is said to us, and that others understand only about a half of what we say to them. Let me share a few thoughts that will help you become a more effective verbal communicator. These ideas will almost certainly make you a better salesperson.

First, always resist the temptation to answer your own questions. You'd be amazed how often most of us do this! I recently conducted an informal survey at my office on this topic, and learned that people either answer their own questions, or assist in providing answers to their own questions, about *30 percent of the time!*

When a salesman says something like, "How's business? Pretty good?" the customer will almost always agree with him and he'll have learned nothing. A much more effective questioning technique is to ask very direct questions, and then allow the customer to provide the answer. For example, if you say, "How's business?" and wait for the customer to answer, he'll usually tell you his honest impression of how his business is going. Often, his answer will tell you *exactly* how to sell to him.

Next, make very clear and direct statements. I've found that most people make ambiguous, rambling, and hard-to-follow statements when they speak. No professional salesperson can afford the luxury of that kind of ambiguity. In fact, not talking straight or not listening carefully during a sales call can have disastrous results.

Why is this such an important issue for salespeople?

First of all, your customers are usually busy, with many other things on their mind besides your presentation.

Second, you may become so familiar with your product,

and the presentation you've developed to sell it, that you don't take the time you really need to articulate your proposition clearly.

Third, most customers have an instinctive resistance to buying. As you speak, they're often busy thinking up reasons why they shouldn't buy...so they're not actually listening to what you have to say.

Finally, you can become so preoccupied with what you're saying that you don't really listen to what the customer has to say. In a sense, these "conversations" wind up as nothing more than two people talking to themselves. Communication breaks down, and nothing is accomplished.

Self-discipline and practice are necessary before you can truly master the art of communicating your proposition to prospective customers. That same discipline and practice are also necessary before you can truly listen to and understand what your customer is saying to you. To become a practiced speaker, you'll probably have to identify, and then change, the sloppy speech habits you've had all your life. Here again, your commitment to professionalism and your willingness to invest the time and effort necessary to succeed can make all the difference.

Another point to remember: don't get in your customer's face! It's always difficult to listen to what any person has to say if he or she is standing too close to you. Crowding a customer is one mark of an amateur salesperson. Standing back at an appropriate distance to make your points clearly and distinctly is a mark of a professional.

As I've noted before, there's a lot of false information being taught to today's salespeople—information that's not only incorrect, but often counterproductive. One such idea that you often hear today is "Don't use 'harmful' words when speaking to a customer." So, just what are these "harmful" words you shouldn't be using? Well, you'll hear things like this:

Don't ever say "contract...," say "paperwork."

Don't say "buy," say "it can be yours."

Don't say "down payment" or "deposit," say "initial investment."

Now, all of this may seem harmless enough, but before you decide to buy into this idea, I'd like you to consider the following points.

Remember (*always* remember) that your customers are no dummies. They're probably at least as smart as you are. If you think your customers don't recognize double talk when they hear it, either *you're* stupid, or you think your customers are stupid. In either case, it's not a healthy situation for making a successful sale.

Once your customers recognize that you're not talking straight to them on small points, they'll naturally be much less likely to trust you on more important issues. Your ability to evoke trust from your customers is one of the most important characteristics you can possess as a professional salesperson. Never compromise that professionalism by arousing suspicion with euphemisms and misleading words in your presentation.

Remember: The salesperson who talks straight with customers, who treats customers with respect by not trying to manipulate them, and who listens carefully to what customers have to say will always be successful.

CHAPTER 5

Principles of Selling— Part 2

Many people who undertake a career in sales are very successful. The successful salespeople I've met all have many points in common. They plan wisely, study diligently, prepare thoroughly, work tirelessly, and optimistically expect to succeed. These are the salespeople who can earn a high income and find a good job anywhere.

Then, of course, there are those who start a career in sales but do *not* succeed. Instead of planning carefully, they set high and unattainable goals. Instead of studying salesmanship, they work on developing a positive mental attitude. Instead of preparing, they look for easy ways to trick or manipulate their customers into buying. Instead of committing themselves to hard work, they look for products that are relatively easy to sell. When they fail, they blame others for that failure and, in the long run, they give a bad name to the wonderful profession of selling.

What follows in this section is a concise summary of the principles that, if applied properly, will make you successful in sales. They require planning, study, preparation, hard work, and a good attitude. This summary of principles, if applied, could make an important contribution to the success of most salespeople.

In the Bible, you can find a reference to people who have "itchy ears." These are the people who always want to hear something new. Salespeople, I've found, tend to be like that. Many of them are constantly reading books, listening to audiocassettes, and attending sales seminars in quest of a "magic bullet" that will make their jobs easier.

If you're looking for real success in sales, start right here! The principles contained in this book, combined with hard work, will help you become a successful, highly paid salesperson. Get started now!

1. PRODUCTS OR SERVICES

Select a product or service to sell that you believe in. Be sure that *you* are firmly convinced that the value of the product or service exceeds its price.

Never sell a product or service you don't believe in. Select a product or service that is wanted or needed by enough people to make selling it profitable.

Avoid being sidetracked by ill-conceived schemes or sales scams.

Remember that products that are either "pre-sold" or that are easy to sell always offer little financial remuneration. Conversely, products that are difficult to sell offer significant financial reward.

Select a product or service that requires study, planning, imagination, and work in order to sell it. Then, expect to be paid handsomely for selling it.

Select a company to represent that you can trust and be proud of.

Once you've found a company you can be proud of, be loyal to it. Remain loyal for as long as you are associated with the company.

Remember that your success doesn't depend on the number of opportunities you have, but rather on seizing an opportunity that's presented to you, and making the most of it.

2. PREPARATION

Learn everything you possibly can about your product or service. Study its features, applications, benefits, unique characteristics, construction. Study its history, and learn about its future.

Remember that the only reason anybody ever buys anything is
value— the benefits that the product or service offers. Master
the art of convincing your customers that they'll receive the
desired value or benefits from your product or service.

Understand that every customer wants to do business with a
professional. Your customers don't expect to know what's
best about your product or service...they want and expect *you*
to know that. Make yourself into the professional your customers want you to be.

People enjoy doing business with important, successful people.
Always dress your best, and strive to look as rich, as important,
and as knowledgeable as you possibly can.

The sales profession is unkind to those who are unprepared.

The true sales professional never stops learning.

3. ATTITUDE

Your determination will ultimately make the difference between
success and failure in sales.

Your customer's disposition is a reflection of your own disposition. You can change his or her attitude by changing your own.

Your customers know nothing about your personal situation or
your circumstances. If you're a salesperson, you are also an
actor. Play any role you want to play!

If you're having financial or personal problems, or are having
difficulty adjusting to a sales career, don't try to convince
yourself that things are great by manipulating your attitude.
Make your plans, study your product and sales approach, prepare yourself, and work hard until things *are* great.

Make certain that you're always more interested in helping your
customers by doing a professional job than you are in earning
your commission.

4. SETTING GOALS

Set realistic goals. Having set them, do whatever is necessary to
meet those goals.

Never set goals you know you can't attain. That will only get you accustomed to failure.

Establish short-term goals for the next week and the next month. Set long-term goals for the next year. *Always* make sure that you achieve your goals!

Move from victory to victory by setting and attaining higher and higher goals.

5. MANAGING FINANCES

The number one reason why *good* salespeople fail in this profession is poor financial management.

Wise salespeople are misers with their money until they're well established in sales and are well off financially.

Invest in your profession. Use your money to buy good clothes, a decent car, and a briefcase to enhance your professional image.

Understand and accept the fact that selling will always be a "feast or famine" business. Be sure to keep what you earn during the "feast" to help see you through the "famine."

Money in the bank for a salesperson is as important as inventory in the warehouse for a businessperson.

6. FAMILY INVOLVEMENT

The number two reason why *good* salespeople fail is lack of co-operation from members of their families.

Enlist your family's help as you plan, study, prepare, and commit yourself to your career.

Never criticize your product, your employer, or your coworkers to your family.

7. WORK HABITS

Work however many hours it takes for you to succeed.

Never be late for work or for a meeting.

Never let family, friends, or other circumstances outside the sphere of your professional life infringe on your work time.

A truism: If most salespeople would work the hours they *should* work for just five years, they could afford to work the hours they *do* work for the rest of their lives.

Commit yourself to working the number of hours it takes for you to become the number one producer in your company.

Develop a work schedule that will ensure your success. Then, obey it slavishly until you succeed.

Be a team player. Take every opportunity that presents itself to help your manager.

Take every opportunity to work with other salespeople, especially the superstars. Learn your trade and work habits from winners and you will be more likely to become a winner yourself.

8. IN THE FIELD

Customers may evaluate you in terms of superficial characteristics such as your age, gender, or race, but that will *not* cause them to buy or not buy. Only *value* and *benefits* cause them to buy.

Every personal liability can be turned into an asset. By the same token, assets can, if not handled properly, become liabilities.

Be sure to listen to your customers. They'll usually tell you what you need to know to complete the sale.

When customers agree to listen to your presentation, they *want* to be sold to, *expect* to be sold to, and *deserve* to be sold to.

When the customer offers anything to you, accept it. The best way to ingratiate yourself with a prospective customer is to let him or her do you a favor.

Customers will listen to you more readily if you look important, rich, and professional...but they'll only ever buy from you when the value of the product or service you're offering exceeds the price.

Customers like straight talk. Don't try to trick them...*inform* them. Don't try to manipulate them...*build value.* Whenever you trick a customer into saying yes on insignificant points, all you really do is trick yourself. You will force your customers to say no when it really counts.

Never try to "sell yourself" in order to sell the product or service you have to offer. Make your customers want your product or service so badly that they'll try to please *you* to get a better deal.

Don't try to find a convenient time for your customer to buy. Create a selling situation in which it is always to your customer's advantage to *buy now*.

Never try to isolate your customer from his or her business, family, or friends out of fear that distractions will disrupt your presentation. *Welcome* distractions, and turn them to your advantage. Your prospect's customers, family, and friends will usually help you by encouraging the customer to buy. After all, they can afford to be big spenders when your product or service doesn't cost *them* any money!

Don't restrict yourself by waiting until customers are ready and able to pay for your product or service. Create so much value and urgency that they'll rearrange their priorities to come up with the money, here and now.

Don't attempt to sell to your family, friends, church, club, or lodge. Don't capitalize on your personal relationships. Sell your product or service based on the merits it has to offer, and on your own ability to sell.

Don't bore your customers. Tell them only what they need to know about construction and features, then spend your time selling *value* and *benefits*.

Don't lower your price in the hope that this reduction, in and of itself, will make the sale for you. Lower your price *only* to help your customer *buy now* what he or she would otherwise buy at a later time.

Don't try to get your customer to agree with you on the points you make. One sure mark of an amateur is a constant need for reassurance and approval. A professional, on the other hand, is able to state his position clearly, with no concern one way or the other whether the customer agrees with him or not.

The best time to call on your customers is when they're busy. When your customer is busy handling his own business, serving customers, and earning money, he feels prosperous.

Calling on customers when they're busy lends importance to the visit. Work to convince customers that what you have to say is so important that they should make the time to listen to you. When you do this, you'll establish a base of value in the customer's mind that starts you building toward the sale.

When your customers are busy, it adds urgency to your offer.

A well-crafted, carefully practiced presentation should *always* be more interesting than any distractions that might occur in your customer's place of business.

Remember that driving and dreaming isn't working. Working, for a real salesperson, means engaging the customer and taking action to make the sale.

9. PRESENTATION

Every good sales presentation has three fundamental characteristics:

1. It tells customers everything they need to know about the product or service so that they can make an intelligent decision.

2. It builds enough value into the product or service to motivate the customer to buy the product or service you're offering.

3. It gives your customer a logical reason to buy *now*.

Presentations should always be designed to inform the customer about your product or service. They should never try to manipulate customers into doing or saying anything they don't want to do or say. Instead, they should allow your customers to reserve their judgment while the salesperson builds both value and urgency.

Presentations should always communicate information about the quality and features of the product or the service. However, this information should serve only as a platform upon which you can build value.

Action on your part, like action scenes in a movie, can warm your customer up to your presentation and can help put him or her into a buying mood.

Customers almost always must be *sold to.* We all have a natural reluctance to part with our money, even when we clearly need something. That's why salesmen are, and always will be, in demand.

Study your presentation until you can deliver it perfectly and convincingly. Make sure your customer thoroughly understands *all* aspects of your presentation.

Practice your presentation until you can deliver it flawlessly. Don't ever settle for mediocrity.

Master your presentation until you can deliver it clearly, accurately, and convincingly. Every word, gesture, and movement should be choreographed to achieve the maximum impact possible. Also, be sure that the props, printed materials, or other items that you use during your presentation are applied smoothly and efficiently.

Once again, "all the world's a stage," and the salespeople are the actors. Some people have low-paid bit parts. Others have highly paid parts as Oscar-winning superstars. Unlike professional actors, we're able to select for ourselves the parts we want to play! Why not go for the top of the bill?

10. OBJECTIONS

Good salespeople hear few objections.

Answering objections will not sell a product or service. Building value is the only thing that ever makes a sale.

Every objection presented by a customer can be transformed by the salesperson into a reason to buy.

The more your customers consider the value and benefits of your product or service, the less important their objections become.

A carefully developed presentation can build so much value into a product or service that even customers who *have* objections will disregard them.

You, as a salesperson, can never answer for your customer's spouse, landlord, accountant, partner, or board. You can't solve his financial problems or any of the other issues he may present as objections to your presentation. You can, however, make your customer want your product or service so badly that he'll ignore or forget about these problems.

11. EVOKING TRUST

You'll be trusted by your customers if you are completely trustworthy yourself, and if you *expect* to be trusted.

If you ever attempt to manipulate your customers on small points, you'll inevitably cause them to mistrust you.

12. PRICE

Customers buy *only* when they believe that the value of a product or service exceeds its cost.

Whenever customers tell you that a price is too high or that they don't have enough money, they are *really* telling you that you haven't built enough value into the product or service you're offering.

The average salesperson drops his or her price too soon, too often, and by too much.

Whenever you lower your price, you automatically lower the value of your product or service in your customer's eyes. Every time you lower a price to create urgency to buy, be sure that you also simultaneously raise value in order to compensate for the lowered price.

Raise value generously; lower prices as sparingly as possible.

Customers can't know for certain if they'll be ready or able to buy until they have all the facts, and have considered all the benefits of any product or service.

The more customers consider the value and benefits of the product or service you're offering, the more capable they are of finding a way to afford it.

The average salesperson tends to place too much emphasis on the price of a product or service, and not enough emphasis on the value and benefits offered by that product or service.

When customers want a product or service badly enough, they'll *always* find a way to meet your price.

When you're broke or desperate to make a sale, it's difficult to tell yourself that money is no problem. If you unintentionally communicate your anxiety to a potential customer, he or she will become "infected" with your own attitude. Chances are, the customer will tell you that he can't buy your product because *he's* broke. Remember that as a salesperson, you're also an actor. Play the role of the millionaire salesperson, and you'll soon discover that everyone will be able to afford the products or services you're selling!

13. CONTROL

Salespeople who are in control of themselves have little trouble controlling others.

Self-confidence is the best method of controlling others.

Great salespeople master the art of controlling customer interactions with their words and their voice.

Study the way you walk, your posture, and the gestures you use to help you remain in control at all times during your presentation.

Keep your focus on your objectives. Don't ever allow yourself to be sidetracked or distracted.

Dress as though you believe that you're important, and your customer will believe that you *should* be in control.

Practice speaking with authority.

14. CLOSING

The only time to close any sale is when the customer knows everything he or she needs to know to make an intelligent buying decision, and is ready to say yes.

Closing a sale almost always means giving the customer a special deal to do business *now*. The customer, however, will never believe that you're giving him a special deal if he or she doesn't see how you will also benefit from the transaction. As you're building value for your customer, you must also build value for yourself to justify your special offer.

Show your customer why buying your product or service *now* is a logical and sensible thing to do. Show him or her why *not* buying now is illogical and foolish.

A lower price won't make customers buy something they don't want, but a lower price *will* motivate them to buy something now that they may be planning to buy later.

Customers almost always need a logical reason to buy now on *your* terms rather than later on *their* terms.

When customers are convinced that the value of your product or service exceeds the price you're asking, they'll buy. The more you raise value, the easier it will be to close a sale.

Never be more anxious to sell than your customer is to buy.

Remember that closing a sale is payday for most salespeople. It's in your best interests, therefore, to master the art of closing.

15. BUILDING VALUE

Order takers sell their products or services by talking about construction and features. They describe things like reliability, durability, and the unique characteristics of a product or service and the company behind it. Then, they try to sell by manipulating the price. Order takers are boring.

Good salespeople make clear and straightforward presentations. They tell their customers everything they need to know about the product or service in order to let them make an intelligent buying decision.

Good salespeople concentrate on finding out what the customer values. They can then incorporate that information into their presentation. This is the essence of quality salesmanship. Good salespeople make a lot of money.

Great salespeople do everything that good salespeople do, but they always go one step further. They cause the customer to see, feel, and experience himself enjoying the benefits of the product or service. Great salespeople are highly paid professionals.

The super salesperson is a great actor. Once he has the customer perceiving himself enjoying the benefits of his product or service, he then lets the customer see his friends, family, and peers watching him enjoy those same benefits. The super salesperson taps into the customer's ego.

Customers will buy almost anything it if appeals to their ego. They will lose their normal reluctance to buy. Also, customers will make almost any sacrifice in order to satisfy their egos.

An ego-based purchase isn't given the kind of scrutiny that is normally given to buying decisions. Purchases don't have to make complete "dollars and sense" when the ego is involved in the decision-making process.

Super salespeople can sell anything, at any time, to anybody, for any price. As a result, super salespeople can make as much money as they want to make.

CHAPTER 6

Principles of Selling in Action

The stories you'll read in this section are all true. The names have been changed to protect the guilty; the innocent need no protection. They are just a small selection of the adventures that my salespeople and I have experienced over the years. As I've said before, life is an ongoing adventure for good salespeople.

The fun is just one of the hidden but very enjoyable benefits of the selling life. As you read these stories, share the sense of fun with me. Also, keep the following points in mind:

1. Look at the many different kinds of adventures you can have. Consider all the fun and the satisfaction, along with the personal rewards that selling can offer you.

2. Look for the selling principles described earlier in this book, and see how they're applied in a variety of situations. Remember that *knowledge* by itself is not power; power is the *application* of knowledge in the real world.

3. Always remember that even the most seemingly impossible situations can be turned into successful sales. A good salesperson should be able to sell to almost anyone.

These days, many different types of people think of themselves as salespeople. This group ranges from chief executive officers of corporations who earn vast sums of money to people who are going from door to door and struggling to make ends meet.

These people are my heroes. They ask for nothing but a chance to compete. They are the chance-takers and the dreamers. They are willing to face overwhelming odds as they sell their products and services. Without these salespeople and the independent businesspeople to whom they sell, this country would grind to a halt. These people make our country great, keep our factories running, and their spirit keeps our nation free.

The principles that are illustrated in the following stories will help any one of these people become more successful in sales. With these stories, I'd like to draw everybody's attention to direct sales, the greatest profession on earth. Selling can be an exciting, fun-filled, rewarding career...one that offers the quickest path to advancement of any profession. This is true, however, only for those who prepare, study, practice, and commit themselves to hard work.

Selling is a career for those who strive to reach new heights. Like a dedicated athlete, a successful professional salesperson is always reaching toward his or her goals, achieving them, and then setting higher ones. Someday, in fact, I'd like to organize a "Salespersons' Olympics." Imagine it! Salespeople would gather from all across the nation. They would compete against each other out there on the "playing field"—the open marketplace.

We then select the top thousand, the top one hundred, and then the top ten...all on national television! We crown the top salespeople, publicize their adventures and income, and praise them for their heroic achievements. Children all over the country will turn to their parents and say, "Mom and Dad, I want to be a salesperson when I grow up!"

HAVING FUN

One summer day when I was scouring the boonies of Alaska for prospects, I met a grizzled old-timer named Stoney. Stoney owned a bar twelve miles down a dead-end road far from anything you or I would call civilization. Normally, I tell my customers that thousands of people pass by their locations every day, and that my sign will help attract the attention of all these people. In Stoney's case, I had to modify this a bit. I said, "Stoney, there's somebody passing by this place once every week or so...it's *necessary* for us to get their attention!"

Stoney was an old sourdough who'd seen it all. He sat on his stool and sipped on a glass of whiskey throughout my presentation. His stubbly beard, redneck cap, rolled-up sleeves, and faded Levis gave him the unmistakable stamp of a "good ol' boy." I sold Stoney a small sign, had a few drinks with him, swapped some fishing lies, and left.

Ten years later, I took a fishing trip to Alaska. I found myself in Stoney's territory, so I decided to stop in at his bar for a visit. When I walked in, there he was, sitting on that same stool. He was wearing the same shirt, cap, and dirty Levis. He was sipping slowly on a glass of whiskey. It was as though he had never moved since I'd first met him ten years before.

As I approached the bar, Stoney lifted his head, set eyes on me, and grinned. "Hi, Allard," he said. Well, we talked, laughed, and drank for a while. I then asked Stoney if I could take a picture of him standing next to the sign I'd sold him ten years before. "What do you want a picture of me for?" he asked. "Stoney," I said, "I've become famous since I sold you that sign. Boy, you might wind up on the cover of *Life* magazine!" Stoney stood up and smoothed the wrinkles out of his Levis. Then he spoke. "Mr. Allard, do you suppose I could get in the *Denver Post* instead? Everybody knows me in Denver."

JIM'S TIRE STORE

One of my more unusual early sales occurred in Charleston, West Virginia. I was making my presentation to a young man named Jim who owned a tire store. He patiently listened to everything I had to say, but he definitely wasn't in a buying mood. I did everything I could to get Jim to see the value of the sign I was offering. I told him that it would pay for his rent and his overhead. I told him that it would bring in new customers. Nothing worked. Finally, after Jim told me more about himself and his family, I came up with an idea that I thought might help make the sale.

I took Jim outside and pointed up to the front of his establishment. I said, "Jim, look up there. Now, imagine your mother driving up here with her Sunday school class. She'll point up there with pride and say, 'That's my boy Jim's place.'" Jim looked silently at the front of his store, and then turned to me. "Write it up," he said.

As I'd talked to Jim and listened carefully to his story, I'd learned that his mother had helped him through many difficult times. Jim was proud of his mother, and it was quite evident that he sincerely wanted her to be proud of him. Jim didn't hesitate or consider the cost of the new sign because he saw that it would give his mother the opportunity to feel good around her friends and associates.

I've used this technique in many different ways to sell hundreds of signs. Sometimes I'll say to the customer, "You remember that girl in high school? You know, the one who said you wouldn't amount to a hill of beans? Some day, she'll be driving by here with that guy she married. She'll look up here and say, 'I could have had that man.'" Of course, there might not be an old high school sweetheart, but I've found that there's always someone—an ex, a peer, a rival, or a sibling—who the customer wants to imagine shaking his or her head in admiration or envy as they admire the purchase.

This appeal to the customer's sense of self-esteem can work in any number of ways. The key is to dig in and find the way to make this work for you in each selling situation. The champion salesperson, like a champion boxer, will always find some way to win.

STANLEY'S USED CARS

One day when I was working in Nashville, Tennessee, I got a phone call from Matt, one of my salesmen. He told me that he'd just wrecked his car. He needed a car to work, so I said that I'd help him find a replacement vehicle. We located a used car lot not far from our motel and pulled in. Matt smiled as we drove up close to the office. "I pitched to this guy just yesterday," he said. "He liked the sign all right, but he doesn't have any money right now." I responded, "Well, let's make sure."

We met Stanley, the owner, and introduced ourselves. He remembered meeting Matt and greeted him with a smile and a handshake. I asked him if he'd really liked the sign, and if he really didn't have the money to buy it. He said yes to both questions. I then made my initial proposal. "Well," I said, "if you'll do some things for me, I'll use your place as a showcase location. I'll pay most of the cost of the sign, and I'll buy that Plymouth over there if you'll give me a good deal on it." This got his attention. He agreed to take another look at what we had to offer.

I told Stanley that he needed to make an impression on the people who were passing by his lot every day. We went outside and took a look at his layout. I noted that there were many large oak trees located throughout his property. I suggested to him that he whitewash the tree trunks up to a height of about five feet. He agreed to do it.

At that point, I had him look across his lot and imagine customers coming by and seeing those whitewashed trees. I then told him to clean up the lot and the adjacent hillside until it looked as pristine as a golf course. He agreed to do that as well. Next, I had him visualize the impact that these changes would have on the people travelling by this location. I could see that Stanley's dreams were slowly coming back to life.

I then suggested that he wax all the cars he had in stock and line them up along the perimeter of the lot. He agreed. I said he should lift all the hoods on those cars one day, and then turn them around and lift the trunks the next. He agreed to do that as well. In fact, he was now telling me that he'd been planning to do these things all along, but just hadn't gotten around to it yet! As I got him to think more about these things he'd been "planning to do," he got more and more excited. At that point, I designed a sign for him, and made it an integral part of that revitalized dream.

As all salespeople know, there's a lot of give and take in almost every sale. After Stanley began dreaming and developing his plans, with my sign securely lodged within those plans, I gave him a logical reason to buy then and there. I sold the sign for a lot more than Matt had quoted the day before, plus we got a fantastic deal on the car. The difference almost paid for the car. How did I do it? There were two reasons. First, Matt had tried to sell the customer something that he didn't want by lowering the price. That approach never works. If a customer doesn't want something, it's not a bargain at *any* price! I had rekindled Stanley's dream, and made my sign a vital part of that rekindled dream. I then gave him a logical reason to make a decision to buy now.

Second, I created a powerful inducement for the customer to agree to the purchase by agreeing to take something on trade. In so doing, I was able to build a lot of value into my own product while also taking advantage of the customer's desire to sell me *his* product. He was motivated to treat me differently because I was more than just a salesman—I was also a potential customer. I saw clearly that it would be much easier to sell a sign for two thousand dollars along with a one-thousand-dollar car than it would be to sell the product for two thousand without taking the car. This is a technique that can be incorporated into the sale of almost any product or service.

AUSTIN'S LIQUOR

One day in Nashville, Tennessee, Jimmy Thumper and I were trying to sell a sign to the owner of Austin's Liquor Store. Austin wasn't in a buying mood. He told us that he already had a sign—the one that came with the place when he bought it from the previous owner, Ozzie. The old sign, reading "Ozzie's Liquor," would be fine. Besides, he was broke. Well, as I've said, I've never met a man who was too broke to buy something that he really wanted and needed, so I decided to sell Austin a sign.

After my presentation and several "no" responses from Austin, I decided this called for stronger measures. This guy *really* needed a sign. I tried a different tactic. I said, "Don't you ever worry about how much ribbing your kids must take? I'll bet they tell their friends that their daddy owns a liquor store, and you know what the other kids say? I'll bet they say, 'Austin doesn't own *Ozzie's* Liquor...Austin's just a clerk in Ozzie's store!' See, the sign says Ozzie's. Little kids would never believe that Austin owns Ozzie's Liquor Store."

Austin acted as though I'd hit him below the belt. "That was a mean shot," he groaned. I kept pushing ahead. I started describing his dear wife driving by with her friends. "She has to tell everyone that her husband works in the liquor store," I said. "She can't tell her friends with pride that she and her husband *own* the store. No one who can read the sign you've got out there would believe her."

I was shameless. I was merciless. I exploited Austin's pride of ownership. I tried to embarrass him into wanting to see *his* name on the business. "You are a cold-hearted man," Austin said to me. Still, I wasn't able to make the sale.

I tried appealing to his patriotism and his community pride. I even asked him to help out a poor, struggling salesman. Nothing worked. Well, the harder you work, the luckier you get, and I finally got lucky. I said, "Austin, remember that old girlfriend...the one who said you would never amount to a hill of beans? Some day that girl is going to drive by here and see your name up on that sign. She'll look up at it and say, 'You know, I could have had that man....'"

Austin's face lit up. "You're right, Mr. Allard," he shouted as he rushed to the telephone. "*She'll* loan me the money!" A short while later, Austin's old girlfriend showed up with the four-hundred-dollar deposit. Austin made me agree to one condition, though. I had to promise never to tell his wife how he'd gotten the deposit! Ever since that day, I remember Austin when I teach new salespeople that if you push enough buttons with your customers, one is bound to work.

THE BAPTIST CHURCH

Because of my religious background, I often call on churches and Bible stores when I'm selling. One day, Jimmy Thumper and I were making a call on the pastor of a Baptist church. I set about building value immediately. After a short while, I had the pastor, who was named Amos, very excited about having a new sign and seeing all the people looking at it and talking about it.

I told Amos that all those wicked liquor stores had big, lighted signs...why not a church? Amos wanted the sign; I could see that. When I got to the close, however, Amos had a problem—no money. He showed me his checkbook register. His account had a total balance of two dollars. Well, this actor/salesman got an idea.

I shouted, "Moses, what's that in your hand? It's a staff...no, it's turning into a snake! Moses, you can part the Red Sea with that. Moses, with a little bit of faith, you can bring nations to their knees with that thing...you can liberate your people!" Amos was getting the idea now. He became Moses, and started walking around, parting the Red Sea with his checkbook.

I shouted, "Shimgar! Let's kill some Philistines with that oxgoad!" He started killing Philistines left and right. (Those of you who aren't Bible students will have to look up Shimgar in the Bible to understand this metaphor.) I then shouted, "Gideon, come out of that cane break, and let's have a victory!" Amos said, "I'll do it," and signed the contract. He then started writing a check for the amount of the deposit.

Of course, I didn't want a rubber check, so I stopped him and said, "Brother, that's not a good idea." Amos said, "Why?" I told him, "Well, I've got faith and you've got faith, but the owner of my company doesn't have any faith at all. He wants cash." "How are we going to come up with the cash?" he asked. I thought for a minute and said, "Let's call a deacon." Amos decided to give it a try.

The first deacon he called told him that he didn't have any money to give him. Amos was disappointed when he hung up the phone. "Sorry, no luck," he said. I thought for a moment and said, "Amos, let's try this another way. Call another deacon and tell him exactly what I tell you." He agreed to give it another try, and called a second deacon.

I whispered into his ear, "Tell him you have a spiritual emergency. Tell him to get his Bible." Amos said what I told him to say. I went on. "Now, tell him to lay his hand on the Bible." He did. "Now ask him if he has four hundred dollars in cash." The deacon had the money, and agreed to bring it over to help Amos with his emergency. Jimmy Thumper and I had the deposit, and the sale was closed. The pastor got his sign, and everybody was happy.

By the way, Amos and I became close friends, and to this day we still laugh about how he got his sign.

MIKE'S CYCLE SHOP

I was training a pair of new salespeople in Oakland, California one day and was feeling good about the number of signs we'd managed to sell. We walked toward the door of a motorcycle shop with a tattered old sign that said "Mike's Cycles." A big, tough-looking biker wearing a grease-stained Harley Davidson t-shirt was leaning against the door frame. "What do you want?" he growled.

I smiled and said, "I'm looking for the owner of this business...is that you?" He didn't smile back. Instead, he spit on the porch and said, "Yeah, what do you want?"

"I sell big, lighted signs," I said. Mike snarled at me, "I don't want no friggin' sign!" I walked over to him and looked him in the eye. "I know you don't," I said. "That's why I'm here. You see, my boss told me that he'd give me a promotion if I found the meanest bastard in Oakland and sold him a sign. That's you, right?"

Mike smiled slightly. "That's right...but I'm not buying no friggin' sign!" I shrugged and said, "Well, I've got to try, so I'll go get my sample." To make a long story short, I sold Mike a sign. I sold it because *I wanted to sell it,* not because he wanted to buy. There's no real trick to it. You can sell anything if you do it correctly.

THE SHOCK TREATMENT

This technique is a lot of fun, and I love using it. Occasionally, when a customer tells me he or she isn't going to buy, I'll say something like, "The heck you're not. My boss told me that if I call on twenty customers, one'll buy. Well, I've been counting...you're the twentieth...you have to buy!"

Sometimes when a customer says he or she doesn't want to buy a sign, I respond indignantly with, "That's not the issue. I want to *sell* a sign!" Often, they stare at me in amazement and agree to hear my presentation. On other occasions, when a customer seems to be uninterested in my proposition, I'll bet them twenty to a hundred dollars that I can make the sale. I've sold lots of signs that way, and never lost a bet yet.

RONNIE'S VACUUM SHOP

As I developed and fine-tuned my selling techniques, I started seeking out selling situations that were more difficult and more challenging. One of the most challenging ever was a vacuum cleaner shop in Indianapolis. My manager, who was named Steve, and I decided to call on this shop because he needed a new vacuum cleaner, and decided to kill two birds with one stone. After we introduced ourselves to Ronnie, the owner of the shop, he told us that he'd just bought a new sign. In fact, it was still in its crate sitting in the middle of the floor. Here was a challenge, all right. Not only did Ronnie not want a new sign...he didn't want to *hear* about any other sign.

It took a while, but I finally convinced Ronnie to look at what I had to offer, "just so he'd know what was new on the market." I sat my sample on the crate, and proceeded to do my best to sell him my sign. I put on a real show for Ronnie, trying everything

I could think of to get him to buy. I convinced Ronnie that the long-term benefits of using my sign would far outweigh the insignificant fact that he'd spent a little money on another sign he might not use. I built a lot of value in every area that I thought was of importance to this independent businessman.

After a while I noticed that Ronnie seemed to be fascinated by my modest celebrity status. I showed him a picture of my crown and sales awards. It became obvious that he enjoyed doing business with winners. He finally said, "Give me one good reason why I should buy your sign, and I'll buy it." I smiled and said, "Ronnie, the best reason in the world for you to buy is that you'll be buying from me." I again showed Ronnie a picture of me wearing my king's crown.

I told him, "Ronnie, some day you'll be an old grandpa bouncing your little grandbaby on your knee. You'll be bragging to your grandchild, just like we all do. The one thing you'll be most proud of is this sign. You'll point to it and say, "Honey, Lloyd Allard designed that sign. I bought it from him personally." Your grandchild will look up and say, 'Uh-*uh*, grandpa, you're just making that up.' But you'll know in your heart that it's true. You'll know you've got an original."

Believe it or not, Ronnie decided to buy the sign, but only if I'd agree to either put my picture on it or sign it with the message "designed by Allard." I filled out the paperwork for the sale using the crate holding Ronnie's first sign as a writing desk. And, since I'd given Ronnie a good deal on his sign, my manager, Steve, got a new vacuum cleaner to set up housekeeping in Indianapolis.

FLASHING LIGHTED CROSS

One of the most fascinating aspects of being a professional salesperson is the wonderful and interesting people you meet. Every day can be an adventure. Every day you might have the good fortune to meet someone like Dillie.

Dillie is a combination auto mechanic and preacher who owns a garage in Los Angeles. His garage has a big sign that says,

"Give your heart to Jesus, but give your car to Dillie." Dillie is a character that you don't soon forget. His teeth have been replaced by solid gold inlays, both top and bottom. Inlaid in white along the top row of teeth is the word "Jesus." On the bottom row is the word "Saves." When he smiles broadly, which is often, the full message "Jesus Saves" beams from his face. Against Dillie's very dark skin, these white letters on a gold background are quite striking.

Jimmy Thumper and I decided to call at the garage and try to sell Dillie a new, lighted sign. Dillie chatted with us for a while, and finally told us that he wasn't interested in a sign for the garage. He *did*, however, want one for his house of worship.

We showed Dillie our sample and gave him a big build-up about how the new sign would set his church apart from all the others. As we spoke, Dillie smiled frequently, flashing "Jesus Saves." We proceeded through the presentation, showing him the different styles we had to offer. Dillie finally saw something that he really liked. It was a large, flashing sign that we usually sell to places like pizza parlors or hot-dog stands. Dillie loved it. It was just what he wanted.

Dillie grew more and more enthusiastic. He told us that he wanted a 35-foot flashing cross on the top of the church. He wanted the sign to read "I am's what I am's what I am's — The Church of the Divine Salvation in Christ. The Most Reverend Dillie Durham, Pastor." I tried to encourage Dillie to consider a more conventional church sign, but he was fixed on his idea. I suggested that it would be difficult if not impossible to mount the sign onto the church building. Dillie responded with indignation, informing us that he was a certified welder…he'd put the sign up himself!

Well, like all salespeople, I'm interested in making the sale. I like to do good, but I also like to do well. While I never believe that the "customer is always right," I make reasonable accommodations to make a sale. And Dillie was certainly right about one important fact—the sign he wanted would certainly attract attention! I wrote up the order and took his check for one thousand dollars as a down payment and my commission.

Dillie's sign arrived a short time later and, as he promised, he put it in place by himself. It looked pretty good, and you could certainly see it well at night. As I shook hands with Dillie one last time, I told him to give me a call if he ever had any problems with the sign. Little did I know what that casual remark would ultimately mean.

A few months later, Jimmy Thumper burst into my office. "We got a problem," he said. "You remember that big lighted cross we sold a while back?" I told him, "Sure...who could ever forget Dillie Durham and his big cross?" "Well, he just called. It's not there anymore. It fell down in a windstorm and tore a big hole in the roof of the church. On top of that, it's blocking traffic on the street." Yes, I figured we definitely had a problem.

I rushed over to see the damage with my own eyes. Standing out front surveying the scene was Dillie, together with a few parishioners. I walked up to him and said, "Dillie, I understand we've got a problem with the sign." Dillie flashed me one of his trademark smiles and said, "No, brother Allard, we ain't got no problem with that sign. It fell off the church, tore a hole in the roof, blocked the road, and it didn't even break. You want me to write a letter telling people how tough your signs are, Mr. Allard?" "I knew I could count on you, Dillie," I said. Dillie smiled again. "Jesus Saves" never looked better, or meant so much.

In a time when it seems as though everyone is looking for an opportunity to sue everyone else, when everyone seems to want something for nothing, it's heartening to discover that there are people like Dillie Durham out there. This world could sure use more of them! I'm sure that I'd never have met this wonderful human being if it hadn't been for my chosen profession. What a great job it is! What tremendous adventures you can have every day! What great people make up this great country!

THE PATEL MOTEL

A while back Jimmy Thumper and I were travelling from Los Angeles to Nashville selling signs and generally having a good time. We stopped off in Las Vegas for a little partying and lots of selling…or vice versa. After this "R and R" (Rest and Remuneration) we headed east. We were making several thousand dollars selling each day, and we were having a great time. One night we stopped at a motel in Amarillo, Texas. The following morning, we had breakfast in the restaurant attached to the motel. The man who managed this restaurant had the appearance and accent of someone who had been born and raised in India.

As he walked by us, I stopped him and asked, "Excuse me, sir. What is your name?" He answered, "I am Mishra Patel. Can I help you?" I've always had good experiences doing business with people from India, and they've done well by me. Though they can be tough to sell to, I've found that they often like large signs that pay very good commissions. Negotiating with these people can be a long and arduous process. However, I've found that Indians are open minded and will give fair consideration to almost any new product or service that might help their business.

"I'm a sign man, Mr. Patel," I said. He brightened. "Ah, yes, I need a sign," he said. That was all I needed by way of an invitation. I launched into my presentation immediately. It went well, with a lot of give and take. I convinced Mr. Patel that the sign I was offering would bring in enough new business to pay for itself in relatively little time. Of course, I built in an ego factor as well, telling him how all of his relatives who were also in the motel business would react to his sign. Finally, he was convinced that he'd be getting a bargain, and was ready to buy. Then he threw the curve ball. "I tell you what, Mr. Allard," he said. "I will buy the sign, but first I must show this to my older brother."

I was startled. "Mr. Patel, I thought you owned this motel," I said. "I do," he responded, "but out of respect, I must first show it to my big brother." This wasn't part of my game plan. I was heading for Tennessee and not only was I not coming back, I was not staying very long. Not buying now has to mean not buying, period. I had to do something to convince him to buy now.

Very slowly, I packed everything in my briefcase so that he could see I was leaving. Then I shook his hand. I said, "Well, I can't wait around for your big brother, Mr. Patel, but frankly I hope he isn't anything like my big brother."

"What do you mean?" said Mr. Patel with a tone of uncertainty. "Because," I said, "if your big brother is like my big brother, and he finds out what a fantastic offer you turned down, he'll kick your tail all over this parking lot for passing it up." Mr. Patel paused and thought for a moment. He then sat down and wrote out a check to me for eight hundred and fifty dollars.

This story is one light-hearted example of how any objection can be turned into a reason why the customer should buy. It also illustrates another important principle that I live by. As a salesperson, you must *never* be more anxious to sell than your customer is to buy. Don't ever attempt to sell from a position of weakness. Your customers should always be more afraid that they're going to lose out on a great deal than you're afraid of losing out on the sale.

GOOSE HUNT

As Big Mack and I were driving through Arkansas one warm autumn day, we decided to spend the weekend hunting goose. We were both looking forward to the rest and relaxation, but we had one problem—we hadn't brought any hunting gear with us. We decided that our next call had to be a sporting goods store. We found one and sold a sign, earning five hundred dollars in commission. We also took a Remington 1100 shotgun in trade. As we drove on, I started thinking, Maybe I should have a magnum shotgun instead!

We called on a second sporting goods store, and sold another sign. This time, we made four hundred dollars in commission. I got the magnum shotgun I wanted, along with several boxes of shells and a fancy pocket knife for Mack. By this time we were feeling pretty good, and our anticipated hunting trip was becoming more and more appealing. Mack decided we still weren't ready, though...we needed a boat.

We sold a third sign at still another sporting goods store. This time, we made another four hundred dollars and got our little boat, along with a trailer. For good measure, we also got a case of Ducks Unlimited shotgun shells. As night fell, we totalled our single-day earnings: We'd made thirteen hundred dollars in commissions. We'd also taken in trade two shotguns, shotgun shells, a knife, a boat, and a boat trailer. We were now ready for some serious goose hunting!

Imagine yourself driving anywhere you want to go and making commissions that total anywhere from a few hundred to a few thousand dollars a day. Imagine yourself being able to pick up almost anything you happen to take a fancy to in trade. Professional salespeople have an incredible life of freedom and fulfillment available to them…if they know how to take advantage of the potential this profession offers. I, for one, love it and plan to savor every minute of it.

TALKING TO THE DEAD

One day, I called on a flower shop in Elkhart, Indiana. I spoke to a woman behind the counter who seemed to be the owner of the shop. I noticed she had a wedding band on, so I asked her if her husband was involved in the business. She told me that her husband had died. "Well," I said, "you're definitely the one I want to talk to, then."

I showed the woman a sample of a sign and told her how much money it would make for her. I built value and drew her a rough sketch of what I had in mind for her shop.

She seemed like a fine person, and I gave her a good show. As I went along, I started to feel good about where we were headed. This looked like an easy sale. She agreed that she needed the sign and that it would make her a lot of money.

I asked for the order, and she caught me completely by surprise by saying, "I think this is a good idea, but I have to ask my husband first." "I thought you said your husband was dead," I replied. She said, "Yes, he is, but I talk to him every night at midnight. I never do anything without his approval," she said with finality. As I started leaving, I thanked her for her time and said, "Well, tell your husband I said hi." She said, "I like the sign. How do I get in touch with you if my husband approves?" As you know, I never make callbacks, and at this point, I'd decided I wasn't going to sell her anything. I said, "Ask your husband for my phone number. After all, he knows all the answers."

Yes, you're right...I didn't make the sale. But I think that woman may have learned something about talking to the dead. It's very difficult to get any hard information out of those folks...things like addresses and telephone numbers, for example. Of course, if I ever hear a soft voice whispering, "Go back to Elkhart," I plan to break my own rule and make that flower shop my first callback!

BILL'S GROCERY

One time, I called on a small grocery store near Columbus, Georgia. After I introduced myself to the grizzled old man behind the counter, he said, "You must be some kind of durn fool trying to sell signs around here. This is the poorest county in America." Without waiting for a response from me, he pulled out a wad of newspaper articles that supported his view that this was, indeed, the poorest county in America. I thanked him for his advice, and bought a bottle of orange juice. We drank some juice together, and talked on for a while.

It was a beautiful day, and I felt warm and comfortable. Bill was a great old guy who talked for a long time about the history of the area. He seemed to be quite proud of the region in which he lived, even though he was so firmly convinced that the area was drenched in poverty. I decided not to try to sell him anything. I didn't want to spoil the moment. However, I did have to chuckle to myself a little as I walked out the door. You see, I knew something Bill didn't know. I had arrived in this county two days earlier, and had already earned over three thousand dollars in commissions. Regardless of Bill's convictions, I had already confirmed one of my basic ideas about selling—a good salesperson can make a good living anywhere.

TOM'S TRANSMISSIONS

Just down the road from Bill's grocery store, I called on a dilapidated old transmission repair shop. This shop was housed in an old garage that leaned to one side. The structure was propped up tentatively by a big wooden pole. I introduced myself to the owner, a classic "good ol' boy" who was wearing bib overalls and chewing tobacco.

I told him that I sold signs, and that he needed one. Tom spit a shot of dark juice onto the ground and said, "Hell, boy, I don't need no sign. Everybody in this county knows me. You want to get your car fixed right, you've got to come to Tom. You ain't got no other choice." I smiled and said, "Tom, that's probably true, but you still need a sign. Have you ever heard of Aamco Transmissions?"

Without losing an ounce of his poise, old Tom spit once again and roared back a response that I've quoted hundreds of times since. "Hell, boy," he said, "more to the point, has Aamco Transmissions ever heard of *me*? I've been in this business longer, do better work, and know more about transmissions than any of those guys. They should be coming down here to learn how to fix a transmission from Tom."

I should have just given Tom a free sign. I was more entertained talking to him and the grocer, Bill, than I ever have been watching a Broadway play or Vegas show. Life is sweet if you allow yourself to interact openly with other people. Salespeople simply get the opportunity to do it more often than anybody else.

MARQUETTE VIDEO

One day a short while ago, one of our salesmen who was named Thorman called on a video rental store not far from our office. He didn't get the order. When I asked him why, he told me, "Well, the guy wanted the sign, all right, but he didn't have the money." As it happened, I knew a bit about the owner of that store. I knew that he was quite wealthy. Not only did he own that video store, but he also owned a lot of real estate and a big restaurant. I informed Thorman that he'd failed to sell the customer on the value of the sign and that Mr. Marquette *did* have the money. Thorman took issue with my assessment. He told me that he'd been in sales for a long time, and was always able to tell whether a customer was telling him the truth.

This discussion was taking place in front of several members of my sales force, so I decided to turn this incident into a learning experience for everyone. I took Thorman along with three other salespeople back over to Mr. Marquette's store. I told the owner that Thorman had spoken to me about his visit the previous day, and that I felt badly that he wanted a sign but couldn't afford it. I told Mr. Marquette that if he'd do me a big favor and take a second look, I'd make him a very special offer. He paused for a moment, and then agreed.

As I began my presentation, I focused on building value in my customer's mind. I had him imagine looking up at the front of his store and seeing a big, flashing sign with his name on it. I had him visualize all of his friends looking at this sign with pride, and his competitors looking at this sign with envy as they contemplated his success. I had all the customers and co-workers in the store agree that a new sign was essential for the future growth and success of Marquette's video store. In short, I caused this man to want the sign I was offering so badly that he couldn't wait to get it.

When I made my proposition to Mr. Marquette, I made it clear to him that I'd need a lot of help from him. I asked for his promise to help me get new sales leads, and to tell people how much the new sign had helped his business. When I finally gave Mr. Marquette the price, it was over two times higher than the price Thorman had offered the day before. Mr. Marquette exploded. "That guy offered me that same sign for nine hundred dollars with a two-hundred-dollar deposit. Now you're asking twenty-one hundred with a thousand-dollar deposit. What's going on here?"

I quietly told Mr. Marquette this little story. "Mr. Marquette," I said, "one day Pablo Picasso and I went into a hardware store. Each of us bought some canvas for $1.50. Then, we both painted a picture on that canvas. Picasso sold his painting for a hundred thousand dollars. Mine is still worth a buck and a half." I took Marquette's hand, shook it, and said, "Let me introduce myself. My name is Lloyd Allard, and in the sign business, I'm Picasso. Now, do you want a Thorman design representing you out there, or do you want a genuine Allard? The price of an Allard is twenty-one hundred."

Mr. Marquette wanted the sign very badly. He told me all the stories I've heard hundreds of times before…the big bills, the low sales volume…all the usual stuff. I put my arm around his shoulder and said, "Brother, this is one battle you won't have to fight alone. I'll help you pay for that sign. Jimmy, take four hundred dollars off of that deposit, and charge it to me." Jimmy Thumper frowned, and gravely struck four hundred dollars off of the price on our quotation sheet. This was all that Mr. Marquette needed to justify buying the sign that he now needed to fulfill his dream. He pulled a large roll of cash out of his pocket, counted off six hundred dollars, and handed it to me. Why did he do this? It's no mystery…Thorman had lowered his price in order to encourage the customer to buy something he did not want. I had lowered my price slightly *only* so he could justify buying something now that he'd decided he wanted to buy.

REX THE WONDER DOG

I'd now like to relate the story of the most important sale I've ever made. Bobby Lee and I were selling signs in the town of Ripley, Mississippi one day. We had just completed a sale at a small chicken restaurant, and we were writing up the contract. The owner of this restaurant was a charming Southern woman. After the paperwork was completed, she brought us a plateful of terrific chicken, and offered us two cups of fresh coffee.

As we sat there chatting amiably, I looked out the front door. There, begging for chicken from passing customers, was a dirty, shaggy little dog, obviously full of fleas. When I looked at his tough little eyes, I fell in love with him immediately. I quickly thought over my personal history, and realized how much this little dog and I had in common. Fate had obviously dealt him a bad hand, but he'd decided to play the best cards he had.

I asked the woman if she knew anything about that dog, or where he'd come from. She said, "Oh, he's always out there bumming chicken." Apparently he'd been coming around for many days, begging chicken from everyone in sight. The owner shook her head. "He's always running in the street. He's sure to get run over sooner or later." That was all I needed to hear. I had to have that dog, so I decided to "dognap" him. This dog was crafty and wild, however. Bobby and I weren't able to catch him. He soon disappeared into the nearby woods. Still, I wasn't about to give up on him.

We drove back to Memphis, about sixty miles away, and picked up my wife. I explained the situation to her, and we rushed back to Ripley to catch the dog. Sure enough, when we got back to the restaurant, there he was in his usual place, begging food from passers-by.

As I believe I've mentioned earlier, my wife is a very intelligent woman. She decided that the only way to catch this dog was to beat him at his own game. She bought some chicken in the restaurant and offered some to him. Slowly, very slowly, she coaxed him closer and closer. Finally, he moved within range. I leaped, and nabbed him. He didn't like being caught, but soon settled down in quiet submission.

We took this dog home, bathed him, groomed him, and named him Rex. Rex is now a crucial member of our team. He runs around in his little Superman costume and keeps a watchful eye on everything that happens inside and outside our house. No amount of money or personal success could have possibly brought more happiness into my life than Rex has. With my lovely wife, Machiko, my good dog, Rex, and my many successes, I feel that my life is complete. He's just another success story…another story of how anyone can go from rags to riches in sales. There's a valuable lesson in this story. If you read it carefully and discover what it is, please write and let me know.

THE GARDEN RESTAURANT

As I've noted on several occasions, good salespeople are also good actors. They are entertainers, and should always be worth watching and hearing. I've always been of the opinion that if my presentation can't command the attention of my customers over any possible distractions, I don't deserve the order.

When Milt Mannix and I were making sales calls in Providence, Rhode Island, we called on a Greek place called The Garden Restaurant. The owner was a no-nonsense, tough-minded Greek gentlemen named Al. He told us that he didn't have any time to listen to our presentation. In fact, he told me that he had a meeting scheduled with some other salesmen just a few minutes from now. He informed me that I had exactly three minutes to show him my product.

"Darn," I said. "Now I know just how a three-minute egg feels. I can't tell how much time goes by when I'm making a presentation, so when you get ready to stop listening or to buy, stop me, O.K.?" "Sure," he said. "Go ahead."

We soon uncovered the issue that was most important to Al. He was struck by the thought of the other restaurant owners he knew seeing his new image and saying to themselves, "I wish I had something like that for my place." So we caused him to see, feel, and experience all of his friends, family, peers, and competitors seeing him enjoying all the benefits that his new sign would bring.

Then we were interrupted. Two well-dressed salespeople who had the appointment with Al walked in and announced that they were ready to meet with him. I looked at them, and then turned to Al. "Tell you what, Al," I said. "If you want, I'll wait and let you take care of your other business first." "No," Al said, "you just hold on for a second." He then stepped over to the two salespeople and told them that something very important had come up. They'd have to wait for about an hour, or come back later. They opted to wait.

When Al came back to us, we sold him his sign with very little trouble.

Remember:

If you're interesting, entertaining, and professional, you'll always win and hold the attention of your audience.

The best time to sell is when your customer is busy.

When you make your customers want your product or service badly enough, they'll always find a way to overcome their own objections.

STROM'S: YOU BUY, WE FRY

During my early days as a direct salesman, Jimmy Thumper and I did a lot of travelling and selling. We had both been divorced, so we were free to travel and enjoy life as we found it. We also were able to commiserate with one another, and we were in perfect agreement about which sex was *really* responsible for the high divorce rate!

Jimmy was a rough-hewn guy, a little coarse, and he sometimes drank too much. However, Jimmy was also a selling machine. He was able to exercise more control over his customers than anyone I've ever met. He had absolutely no peer when it came to making customers dream about the benefits of owning the product. He was an absolute magician when it came to turning any negative point the customer mentioned into a reason to buy. There are many examples of this special skill I could give you, but consider this one. (Caution—order takers and callback artists! Don't read this story! First, you probably won't believe it, even though it's completely true. Second, if you *do* believe it, it may give you an inferiority complex!)

One time, Jimmy and I decided to drop in on a restaurant where Jimmy had made a sale a year or so before. It was a friendly place that featured fried catfish and chicken as the main items on the menu. This place was owned by a hard-nosed businessman named Strom. When we drove up, Jimmy explained that this account had been a bit of a problem for him. It seemed that when Strom bought his sign, Jimmy had messed up the design a bit. Instead of a picture of a catfish on the sign, Jimmy had called for a picture of a goldfish. Strom, needless to say, was unhappy. Who, other than college kids during the 1920s, ever ate goldfish?

When we went in and located old Strom, we learned that he was opening a new location across town. Jimmy jumped at the opportunity to sell him another sign. As he started presenting his ideas, Strom blew up. "No way, Jimmy!" he said. "You screwed up my last sign. I'm not ready to buy a sign for the other place yet, and believe me, I'm *never* going to buy another one from you!"

Well, believe it or not, we *did* succeed in selling Strom that second sign. Within an hour, we had the contract signed, and we had a six-hundred-dollar cash deposit in our hands. This is how it all went down:

After Strom's outburst, Jimmy said, "Strom, I put that goldfish on that sign for a reason. Think for a minute. Why do people put up signs? To get attention, right? Well, that's what you're getting! Everyone is talking about that crazy guy with the catfish restaurant who's got a goldfish on his sign." Strom stared at Jimmy and asked, "They're talking about me?" "I wouldn't lie to you, man," said Jimmy. "From Nome, Alaska, to New Mexico."

Jimmy was now ready to move ahead. "Strom," he said, "I've got something so hot that I figured you were the only businessman around here that'd appreciate it. I want to show it to you, O.K.?" Strom was now in tune with the program. "O.K., Jimmy, show me," he said.

As Jimmy built value and got Strom dreaming, I could see that old magic happening once again. Strom soon forgot about what he had considered a bad experience with the first sign. He even forgot that he'd ever been mad at Jimmy. Strom wanted to be noticed, and Jimmy gave him what he wanted.

About halfway through his presentation, Jimmy asked a question that he assumed would get a positive answer that he could build on. "How much did that last sign I sold you increase your business, Strom?" Strom's reply was an unexpected curve ball. "Not a bit," he snapped. "Not a doggone bit of change in my business." Jimmy wasn't about to let something like this slow him down. He grabbed Strom's hand and shook it vigorously. "That's fantastic! Would you put that in a letter for me, Strom? Everyone else on this street is on their heinie, and you're still doing just as well as before. This is great!"

By the end of the presentation, Strom was sold. All he needed was a good reason to buy now. He told us, "I left my checkbook at home. Tell you what...you come back in the morning and I'll write you a check then." Jimmy moved closer to him and said, "Are you crazy?" He then pointed at me, and said, "You see this guy? They call him the king of salesmen. He's a one-call closer. If I ever made a callback in front of him, I'd never be able to show my face in this business again! Tell you what...we'll be willing to take cash since we already know you." Strom didn't seem to get Jimmy's little joke. He just nodded and pulled out a roll of fifty-dollar bills. He peeled off twelve, and handed them to Jimmy.

The next time you're making a presentation, remember:

Every negative can be turned into a positive. When value exceeds price, your customer will buy.

For best results, always appeal to your customer's ego.

When customers want your product badly enough, they'll find a way to come up with the money.

MR. TOM'S CAJUN FOODS

The sale I made at Mr. Tom's Cajun Foods is a good example of advanced selling in action. This customer had little interest in the usual reasons that most people buy a sign—to draw customers, make more money, and so on. To sell to this customer, I had to find out what was important to him, and make him visualize himself deriving those specific benefits from my product.

My saga with Mr. Tom started one morning when I was having breakfast with a group of six salespeople in Memphis. As I listened to them talk among themselves, I amused myself listening to them describe how they planned out their workday. Two of them were going to Arkansas to sell. Two others were heading for Mississippi. The other two were going to Jackson, Tennessee, about sixty miles away.

After listening to this for a while, I turned to them and said, "Fellows, I found a fantastic place to sell yesterday. It's a street that looks like virgin territory to me. I'm going over there right now to sell a big sign. Who'd like to come with me and watch?" All six were immediately interested. I got up and walked out the door with all six salespeople in tow. My object was to demonstrate that these people were driving too much, and that the very best territory to work could be the one they were in. It's a lesson most salespeople should learn well. I walked out the door and went directly across the street.

We walked into Mr. Tom's Cajun Restaurant and located the owner, Mr. Tom. He most definitely was not going to be an easy sale. He told me that he had no interest in a new sign because he was doing all the business he could handle. For good measure, he threw in the fact that he'd turned down several sign salesmen during the past year.

Well, here I was with an audience of six salespeople, so I had to produce. I started to ask Tom questions about his business as though I'd lost all interest in selling him anything. Tom told me with great pride that he had introduced Cajun cooking to the Memphis area. Times had been rough at first, but now the taste for Cajun cuisine was sweeping the nation. Tom felt that his business couldn't be better.

As he talked, I got an idea. I said, "Mr. Tom, I've got an idea that I think will help both of us. Please let me show you something." Since I'd listened to Tom's story, he apparently felt obligated to reciprocate by taking a quick look at what I was offering. I geared my presentation to showing Memphis and all the world that Cajun cooking had come of age. I had Tom visualizing all the other restaurant owners in the area looking at his sign with envy. I had him imagining all the new Cajun restaurant owners in town coming in and asking for tips about how to make it in the business. I mentioned that it also wouldn't hurt to show all those folks who'd thought that Tom and his Cajun cooking would fail that he'd succeeded after all. Finally, I said, "Tom, this would be a fantastic opportunity for me to show off my new sign to the public. It would also be a fantastic way for you to show folks just how far Cajun cooking has come. I'm going to make you a fantastic offer."

By the end of my presentation, Tom couldn't wait to buy. In addition to making a sizeable commission on the sale for myself, Tom threw in a special bonus. He invited all of my salespeople in for a Cajun party...on the house! Now, when you invite a bunch of travelling salespeople to a party, you're in for a serious party. We had a great one, and it was all because I decided to walk across the street just to make a point.

If you listen to your customers, they will, more often than not, *tell* you how to sell to them. Listen carefully. The clues may be subtle, but they're almost always there. Don't spend too much time talking yourself. Remember that one of the reasons owls are considered wise is that they keep their mouths shut!

Once you find out what's important to your customer, cause him to visualize himself deriving those specific benefits from the products or services you're offering. To be especially successful, practice having your customer visualize others seeing him as he enjoys the benefits of your product or service. And remember...to justify giving your customer a special offer, you must be sure to point out the benefits that *you* will derive from the transaction. The customer must see what you are getting before he can ever fully believe that you are doing something special for him.

BETTY'S BEAUTY SALON

I recently called on the owner of a beauty salon in an effort to sell her a sign. Betty didn't seem the least bit interested right from the start. As it turned out, she'd pretty much given up on the business, and didn't care much about the future. After a short while, she told me the reason for her depressed attitude. Her husband, it seemed, had recently run off with one of her staff beauticians.

I tried everything I could think of to get Betty to see the value of keeping the business going, but she simply wasn't buying. Finally, I took her out in front of the shop, showed her a sketch of the sign I had in mind, and indicated where I thought it should be mounted on the building. Then I told her to look up and imagine how her ex-husband and that beautician would feel when they drove by and saw that new sign. "He'll see this and say, 'Gosh, it looks like she didn't even miss me.' That bimbo will turn green with envy." She looked at me as a wry smile crossed her face. "Put it on rush," she said.

The salesman who uses some imagination can use endless variations on this process to sell anything.

>   You have to practice...you have to become an actor.

>   You must develop self-discipline...you must learn to *listen.*

>   You must have courage...there will be times when you'll be rejected. You have to be able to accept it, and move on assertively to your next call.

Simply stated, the real sales pro uses this tactic in a variety of ways. If you're willing to work, study, and practice, give it a try!

FLOWER CITY, OR BIG MACK FALLS IN LOVE

As I've mentioned earlier, I believe that direct sales is one of the most exciting professions in the world...and I think I can prove it, too. I often attend managers' meetings, seminars, and business meetings of all kinds. At these meetings, you can meet heads of corporations and executives of every (pin)stripe. If you hang around long enough, you'll find that conversation typically gravitates toward story-telling sessions in which everyone shares their tales of adventure and excitement on the road.

Even if they've been working in executive suites for years, these people love to tell those once-in-a-lifetime crazy stories that can only happen in direct sales.

Probably my favorite story to share in these circumstances is about my friend Big Mack and the time he and I were selling together in Mississippi. Big Mack had something of a split personality. In a barroom brawl, on a hunting trip, or playing football, he was an absolute grizzly bear. When he was around women, however, Big Mack was more of the Teddy variety.

During this Mississippi trip, we decided to call on a flower shop named Flower City. Standing behind the counter was a beautiful young woman with big brown eyes and a fantastic figure. She flashed a smile at Mack. It was soon obvious to me that Big Mack had been smitten. This was love at first sight, all right. Mack introduced himself. She told him her name was Susan. Well, after a few moments, these two didn't even know I was standing there. I'm no fool, so I let Big Mack put on the presentation.

He was brilliant. Mack was as eloquent as any Shakespearean actor, and it was obvious that this young woman was enthralled. Magic of all kinds was *definitely* happening here! Big Mack built a lot of value into the sign, but at the same time he built a lot of value into the idea of Susan getting to know him better, too. Susan was obviously drinking in every word he said. Something wonderful was happening.

It was at just about this moment that Susan's boyfriend walked in. He was kind of a nerd, but he wasn't stupid, and he picked up on the situation right away. He didn't like what he was seeing one bit. He started sticking out his chest and lower lip, almost defying Big Mack to hit him. Then he almost accused Big Mack of trying to steal his girlfriend.

Big Mack smiled gently and, without losing his poise, he set his sample down on the floor. He walked over to this guy and suddenly embraced him in a big bear hug. He lifted him into the air. It looked for all the world as though Gentle Ben were hugging Winnie the Pooh. Big Mack then said in a sad, slow, country voice, "Boy, I'm going to tell you something that's gonna make you a little bit nervous." "What's that?" the guy squeaked, as he struggled to get loose from Mack's iron grasp. Big Mack bent over, kissed him lightly on the ear, and said, "I'm gay." This fellow wiggled himself free in an instant and bolted from the shop. And I'm talking fast…you could have played cards on his coattails.

Well, you can probably guess the rest of the story. Big Mack made the sale, and those two are still talking signs, flowers, and all sorts of stuff I can't really talk about here.

Forget Reynolds, Redford, and Rambo. It's the professional travelling salesperson who's out there living the life of adventure and excitement every day. I'm glad to be one of them, and I'm proud as I can be to be a part of this unique profession.

An Explanation

You're probably wondering about the crown and all this "King of Salesmen" business.

My good friend Sam Golden gave me the crown for breaking several sales records.

My friends have called me the "King of Salesmen" for many years.

Of course, there are a few people who call me other things. Recently, someone called me an egotistical S.O.B. I had to look this up in the dictionary to find out what it meant. No, not the S.O.B. part...I know what that means.

This is what I learned:

Egotistical people think that everything they do is fantastic, and they brag about it 100 percent of the time.

Average people only brag about 50 percent of the fantastic things they do.

Modest people tell about 25 percent of the fantastic things they do.

Now, I only talk about 15 percent of the fantastic things I do...but I do so many fantastic things that it makes me look like an egotistical S.O.B.!

Seriously, I hope you have enjoyed reading this book, and that you got something helpful out of it. If you didn't find anything that you thought was helpful, I hope you thought something in it was funny. If you did neither, all I can say is...I hope you paid for the book!

Thank you,

Lloyd Allard
King of Salesmen